RESEARCHING
PROSPECTIVE
DONORS

Get More Funding
for Your Library

RESEARCHING PROSPECTIVE
DONORS
Get More Funding
for Your Library

SUSAN SUMMERFIELD HAMMERMAN

An imprint of the American Library Association
Chicago   2014

Susan Summerfield Hammerman is a librarian working in the field of fundraising at Northwestern University as a prospect researcher. She has a BA in history from the University of Michigan and an MLIS from Dominican University.

© 2014 by the American Library Association

Printed in the United States of America
18 17 16 15 14   5 4 3 2 1

Extensive effort has gone into ensuring the reliability of the information in this book; however, the publisher makes no warranty, express or implied, with respect to the material contained herein.

ISBN: 978-0-8389-1229-4 (paper).

Library of Congress Cataloging-in-Publication Data
Hammerman, Susan Summerfield.
    Researching prospective donors : get more funding for your library / Susan Summerfield Hammerman.—First edition.
        pages   cm
    Includes bibliographical references and index.
    ISBN 978-0-8389-1229-4 (alk. paper)
        1. Library fund raising—United States. 2. Libraries—United States—Gifts, legacies. 3. Libraries—Endowments—United States. 4. Library benefactors—United States. 5. Information services—United States—Finance. I. Title.
Z683.5.U6.H36 2014
025.1'10973—dc23   2014006069

Book design in the Bembo and Helvetica Neue typefaces by Alejandra Diaz.

♾ This paper meets the requirements of ANSI/NISO Z39.48-1992 (Permanence of Paper).

CONTENTS

Introduction • *vii*

Chapter 1   **Prospect Research Process**   1

Chapter 2   **The Confidentiality Policy**   9

Chapter 3   **Biographical Information**   15

Chapter 4   **Real Estate**   31

Chapter 5   **Finding Salaries and Net Worth**   41

Chapter 6   **Stock Holdings and Compensation
for Prospects at Public Companies**   53

Chapter 7   **Family Foundations**   71

Chapter 8   **Giving to Other Nonprofits and Political Donations**   87

Chapter 9   **Memberships and Affiliations in Clubs
and Other Organizations**   97

Chapter 10   **Capacity Ratings**   111

Chapter 11   **The Research Profile**   123

Appendix: Online Resources and Annotated Bibliography • *141*
Index • *151*

INTRODUCTION

LET'S FACE IT, money is tight and library budgets are cut to the bone. Usually when library budgets are strained, the first thing librarians do is write a grant application and submit it to a foundation hoping that it will be accepted and cover a budget shortfall. However, this may not be the best strategy. It may come as a surprise that the largest source of giving in the United States is made by individuals and not foundations or other organizations. That's right, individuals give more money than foundations. In fact, "in 2011, 73% of all charitable giving in the United States was made by individuals, whereas only 14% of all giving was made by foundations."[1] This means that if your library actively cultivates individuals to increase the number of gifts given to your library, your library's revenues are bound to increase. The most effective way to do fundraising is by asking the wealthiest people affiliated with your library for gifts. "One fund-raising adage is that most nonprofits raise 90 percent of their major gifts each from less than 10 percent of their constituency. For fund-raising goals to be met, donors in the top income groups must be cultivated."[2]

Prospect research will identify who those people are. It is then up to the library director or fundraising staff to build a relationship with those potential donors and cultivate them for a gift.

A quick definition of terms is needed at this point. A *donor* is an individual who has already made a gift to your library. A *potential donor* is an individual who may or may not make a gift to your library and is being cultivated or will be cultivated in the future by fundraisers or the library director to make a gift. A prospect is an individual whom you are researching and is either a donor or a potential donor. All of these terms are often used interchangeably by fundraisers. It is clearer and will help to avoid confusion if you use the term *donor* to refer only to people who have already given to your library.

This book describes how to identify and research prospects for your library using resources that are available to you for free or through subscriptions, many of which your library may already have. This book will help you to identify who to research, what information you will be able to find, where to find it, and how to write it up so it can be used by your library director or fundraisers to cultivate individuals for gifts. You will also learn how to establish a confidentiality policy and how to store information on prospects.

Once you have identified the best people for your library to cultivate, the fundraisers or library director will need to "make the ask." How to do this is beyond the scope of this book. There are many excellent sources that describe the fundraising process for potential donors who have already been identified and how to cultivate prospects to ask for gifts. (An annotated bibliography describing some of these sources is provided in the appendix.) This book focuses exclusively on prospect research—that is, research that identifies which prospects to cultivate and ask for gifts.

This book shows how prospect research is essentially finding and using publicly available information on individuals, particularly information about their wealth and assets. This research is used to help fundraising staff focus their time and attention on the best donors or potential donors so that they can be solicited to make a gift. The information you can find through prospect research helps direct the fundraising staff to the prospects who are most able to make a large gift. Library patrons have a strong connection to their library, and they are often an untapped resource for fundraising. After learning the research skills described in this book, you will be able to assist your library director or fundraisers in getting more gifts from your library patrons. Get ready to start on an exciting and interesting quest for your library to find additional funding!

NOTES

1. *Giving USA 2012: The Annual Report on Philanthropy for the Year 2011 Executive Summary*, Chicago: Giving USA Foundation, 2012, accessed January 20, 2013, http://store.givingusareports.org/2012-Giving-USA-The-Annual-Report-on -Philanthropy-for-the-Year-2011-Executive-Summary-P43.aspx.
2. Cecilia Hogan, *Prospect Research: A Primer for Growing Nonprofits* (Sudbury, MA: Jones and Bartlett Publishers, 2008), 9–10.

Prospect
Research Process

I F YOUR LIBRARY is considering launching a capital campaign, starting or expanding on an annual fund, or simply would like to increase donations to the library, then prospect research will be very useful to help your library fulfill any of these goals. Prospect research is widely practiced by most nonprofit institutions. The purpose of prospect research is to determine who the fundraising staff or library director should cultivate for a gift, by identifying the wealthiest people with a connection to your library. Once those top prospects have been identified, then the fundraising staff or library director will engage those newly identified prospects to facilitate getting a gift from them.

Prospect research is used as a starting point for fundraisers or the library director. Once a relationship has been formed with a donor or potential donor and through discussions with that person, the library director or fundraisers will determine which library project or initiative the prospect is most interested in supporting and the amount to ask for from the prospect.

Does Your Organization
Have a Prospect Research Department?

Many large nonprofit organizations have a dedicated staff who do prospect research exclusively. If you work for a large nonprofit organization with a fundraising staff, first determine if your institution has a department already doing prospect research. If there is a prospect research department, then they will have policies and procedures already in place that you can follow. It is unlikely that the prospect research department will be so overstaffed that they would decline help from the library staff, but it is important to coordinate your efforts.

Presenting Prospect Research to the Library Director

When your library does not have a prospect research staff and you or your colleagues would like to start this process to help your library get more funds, then you will have to present the idea of providing prospect research on the library's prospects to your library director. The most effective strategy to use is to let your library director know that prospect research will identify the wealthiest among your library prospects. Once you have that information, it will allow your library director and fundraisers to focus their attention on those prospects who are capable of giving the largest gifts to the library. This process requires a confidentiality policy in place beforehand, which is described in chapter 2. The library staff who will be doing prospect research will also need a process for saving and storing the research found on prospects. Further information on this is also included in chapter 2.

Informing Library Staff and the Board about Prospect Research

If your library is considering utilizing prospect research as a fundraising tool, this should be an internal decision made by the library director, the fundraising staff (if there is one), and the librarians who will do the research. Part of this process is apprising the library board of this decision. Displaying sensitivity about the confidentiality of the information should be conveyed to the board members, as well as the fact that only basic information about a prospect's wealth will be researched and nothing more. Information gathered through prospect research should be treated as very confidential and shared only with the fundraising staff, the library director, and the staff doing the research, but not the board members. Adopting a confidentiality policy will be part of this process (again, discussed in detail in chapter 2).

Whom Do You Research?

As your library beings the prospect research process, the first thing to determine is whom you are going to research. How to do this research is the focus of this book, so if you have a few prospects in mind to use as test cases while working through each chapter it will be helpful to you in learning how to do prospect research.

You may think that the only criterion is if a prospect is wealthy. While that is very important, of course, the first thing to consider is whether a prospect has demonstrated an interest in your library. That a prospect has an affinity or a potential affinity to your library is the first criteria to use; the next thing to consider is which people within that group are wealthy. To give an example of this: you may give to your alma matter, or your spouse's alma matter or your children's or your parents, but you wouldn't consider giving to a college or university with which you have no affiliation whatsoever unless a fundraiser puts in a lot of effort to convince you to do so. The same is true for your library—it will take a tremendous amount of effort and time on the part of the fundraisers or the library director to get someone who has no connections to your library to make a gift. On the other hand, someone who has already demonstrated an interest in your library (or better yet, has already made a donation to your library) will be much more likely to make a gift—and if they are wealthy, to make a large gift—to your library.

The prospect has to have some association with your library. Keep this in mind when building your prospect pool. The prospect pool consists of the prospects you have researched or will research in the future. It is all of the people who could be solicited for gifts to your library or have already given to your library.

Affiliated Prospects

All libraries should focus first on closely affiliated prospects, which include your board members, donors to your library, library volunteers, members of Friends groups, or members of other groups affiliated with your library and library staff. Everyone within those categories has an affinity for your library demonstrated by their close association with it. The order to research these prospects should be board members first, followed by donors, Friends group members, volunteers, and finally staff.

The suggestion to research staff members may be surprising to you. However, staff members have a very close affiliation with the place in which they work. Many staff members do make donations to their workplace, especially when they are asked to do so. You may wish to focus only on staff who hold the highest position in your library and staff that you speculate might be wealthy. The rest of the staff should be considered for smaller donations to the library. Researching your colleagues is likely to be a touchy subject, so this needs to be discussed with your library director first. Of course, any research that is on your colleagues should also be treated with the highest possible level of confidentiality.

The next and vastly larger pool of prospects is determined in part by the type of library you work for, such as a university library; a public library; a library in a museum, botanic garden or zoo; or a special or private library. These prospects should have some kind of relationship or potential relationship to your library or the parent institution for your library, such as the museum or the university.

These are not hard-and-fast rules, but guidelines to get you started. You may wish to read through all the library types below, as some of those suggestions might be applicable to your library.

Prospects for University Libraries

In addition to those closely affiliated prospects described above, prospects for universities libraries also include the faculty and staff who work outside of the library; alumni of the university; parents of current students; and people who live in the university town or community and are otherwise unaffiliated with the university, but have paid for library privileges (if your library has this arrangement). If your library has events that are open to the public and there is an attendance list, those people who have attended a library event should also be part of your prospect pool to be researched. Another possible set of prospects is donors to other libraries in your community. Your library director or fundraising staff would have to work at getting those prospects interested in your library.

Prospects for Public Libraries

The prospect pool for a public library would include all your library patrons, in addition to those closely affiliated prospects, such as board members. Depending on your library's policies, you may or may not have access to library patrons' information. If not, then the entire town or community would be included in your prospect pool. If you do have access to patrons' records, then focus on that particular group first, followed by everyone in your town or community who does not have a library card. You can also include in your prospect pool anyone who has attended a library event but does not live in your community, if you have access to that information.

Prospects for Museum, Zoo, or Botanic Garden Libraries

Along with closely affiliated prospects, all members of the parent institutions for libraries in museums, zoos, or any other nonprofit library with a parent institution that has memberships should be included in the prospect pool. All donors to the parent institution should also be included in the prospect pool. If your library holds special events, all the attendees at those events who are not members should be included in the prospect pool to be researched as well.

Prospects for Special or Private Libraries

To fill out the prospect pool beyond the board members, donors, volunteers, staff, and members of Friends groups, include all the members of your library. Event attendees should be part of the prospect pool, along with anyone who has taken a class through your library, if your library offers classes or workshops.

Publicly Available Information

Now that you have considered whom to research, the next step is to understand what information you will be able to find on your prospects. You might be surprised by how much information about people is available through public sources. Public sources can give you biographical information, employment and employment history, education, family information, philanthropic giving, property holdings, stock holdings, and even salary information for many people living in the United States. How to find this information is described in detail in later chapters of this book. Those chapters also include worksheets to help you keep track of the information you find; you can use the worksheets to write the research profile.

Prospect research often does not rely on printed sources because the information may not be as current as online sources, so the sources listed in this book are online sources. However, you should use the sources that you prefer and that are available to you through your library.

Private Information

It is as important to know what information is *not* publicly available for the prospects you will be researching as it is to know what you can find. In the United States, you will not be able to find information about a prospect's bank account or unlisted telephone numbers. Stock holdings or salaries for prospects working in private companies or who are not corporate insiders of public companies are not publicly available, unless it is reported in a news source. (Corporate insiders of public companies are the companies' officers, directors, and stockholders who own at least ten percent of the company's stock.) Additionally you will not be able to find information about trust funds for prospects. You also will not be able to find information about a prospect's debt or their net worth unless it was reported in a news source, such as *Forbes*. So, unless any of this information was reported in a news source or told directly by the prospect to your fundraising staff or library director, you will not be able to find it. Some information can be very difficult to find but is not restricted from public sources; for example, there is no specific source to consult to find personal e-mail addresses. Finding family members' names can also be very difficult.

Access to Internal Information

As well as public information, there is information on your prospects that is gathered by your library. Your library will need policies to determine how and if you have access to the information found through library patron records for the purpose of prospect research. Most nonprofit organizations have a separate database to track giving to the organization, and it is in such a database that personal information about donors and prospects is stored, such as home address and spouse's name.

Writing the Research Profile

The information that you find on a prospect externally (through public sources) and internally (through the library) should be recorded. In fact, the purpose of researching a prospect is to turn that research into a written description of what you found on the prospect; this is a *research profile*. A research profile is written for the library director and the fundraising staff to use to solicit the prospect for a gift. Reading it will give the library director and fundraising staff enough background on the prospect to help them determine which library project the prospect may wish to fund and an initial gift range for the solicitation (the amount to ask for a gift). After you've found information on your prospect, you will write up a research profile. (See chapter 11 for a detailed description of what to include in it.) Basically, it includes information that you found on a prospect using public sources: biographical information, employment and employment history, education, family information, philanthropic giving, property holdings, stock holdings, and salary information. Specific suggestions of what to include in the research profile will also be included in each chapter that focuses on finding public information.

Sharing Information Found Through Prospect Research

The goal of prospect research is to help the library director and fundraising staff determine the interests of a prospect and how much the prospect might be able to give to the library. Research profiles are produced for them or any other staff who will be asking a prospect for a gift. As the library director and the fundraising staff are the audience for this research, they should have unlimited access to every research profile on all the library's prospects.

Sharing prospect research with anyone beyond the library director, fundraising staff, and librarians who are doing the research should be done at the discretion of the library director. There should be some reason to share the information that is directly related to researching a prospect or soliciting the prospect for a gift.

Donors who are philanthropic throughout the community are aware of prospect research and aware that they may be the focus of it. That said, prospect research on a nonprofit's prospects usually is not shared with donors, volunteers, or even with library staff who are not directly involved in researching or cultivating the prospect. Technical services or circulation staff should not have access to information found in researching a prospect, unless they did the prospect research or are involved in asking the prospect for a gift.

Sometimes library volunteers or board members instead of the library director ask prospects or donors for gifts for the library. Even if that is the case, the information gathered on prospects through prospect research should not be shared with volunteers, including board members. Although the information you acquire is public, sharing it with volunteers is likely to create an uncomfortable situation for the volunteer or the donor. Therefore throughout this book all references to sharing information found through prospect research and all the examples used in the case studies refer only to the library or fundraising staff who need access to this information.

The Rewards of Prospect Research

This book will give you a solid footing in prospect research. The chapters describing where and how to find information include sources for finding the information as well as case studies to use as practice examples. The purpose of this is to make learning how to find the information as practical as possible. Once you know what information to look for and how to find it, you may wish to use sources other than the ones mentioned in this book, which does not include an exhaustive list of all the possible sources available to you. Additionally, as you become more familiar with the field of prospect research, you may wish to join the professional organization APRA (www.aprahome.org) as well as one of its local chapters. The national organization has an annual conference and offers training in prospect research; the local chapters may offer training as well. In any case, my hope is that with this book in hand, learning prospect research will be easy for you, and perhaps even fun!

The
Confidentiality
Policy

BEFORE YOU BEGIN the process of prospect research, your library must have a confidentiality policy
agreement in place. This policy needs to address what
prospect research includes, in terms of internal information
from the library; which staff will do prospect research; which
staff have access to see the research profiles; whether or not
library volunteers will have access to research profiles; and
guidelines specifying how the research profiles will be stored
to ensure their security and maintain confidentiality. This
policy should be written and signed by everyone who will
be doing prospect research and everyone who will be reading
research profiles before any research is begun.

The "Creepy" Factor of Prospect Research

Prospect research at first glance can seem a little creepy. After
all, you are researching information about people's lives and
wealth for the purpose of soliciting donations to your library.
Nevertheless, it is all perfectly legal and ethical because all
the information you find is public. Most nonprofit institutions conduct prospect research, as it is an integral part of
fundraising; nonprofit institutions rely on donations to sur-
vive. Think of a world without philanthropy! Just as donors
need to find worthy causes, worthy causes need donors. Prospect research is the first step in doing this important work.

As you might imagine, it can be an odd feeling to help
a library patron at the reference desk whom you have researched. However, librarians are well practiced in not di-

vulging confidentiality information. Just as you would never reveal to a parent what their teenage son is reading, you of course cannot reveal that you have researched a library patron—certainly not to the patron, and not to your fellow librarians either, unless they have also signed the confidentiality policy. So, although this is by no means the most important reason to have a confidentiality policy, it is one of the reasons. The policy reinforces the idea that the librarians doing the prospect research, the library director, and the fundraiser have respect and consideration for the library prospects and the information about them. The prospects are not walking dollar signs, but potential donors who will be making gifts to a very worthy cause—your library. You are not snooping, spying on, or stalking your library patrons; rather, you are trying to help your library get more funding. This is the purpose and the goal of prospect research.

Legal Issues

There are legal issues with storing and accessing particular kinds of information, such as social security numbers. This is not the kind of information that you will find through prospect research using public sources. However, your library director may plan to store your public prospect research materials in the same place as other confidential documents that do have legal requirements for storage. If you use internal information from your library that does have privacy laws protecting that information, you must ensure you are compliant with the law. Your library should already have policies in place for any information protected by privacy laws, so if you continue to follow those policies, you should be fine. Refer to your own library policies, the Center for Democracy and Technology's website (https://www.cdt.org/privacy/guide/protect/laws.php), and the American Library Association's standards and guidelines (www.ala.org/offices/oif/iftoolkits/toolkitsprivacy/privacypolicy/privacypolicy) to find more information on this subject, which falls outside the scope of this book.

Defining What is Included in Prospect Research

Of course, all relevant public information will be included in prospect research. It is important for your library director to decide how information that is internal to the library will be handled. The first thing to do is determine what is included in prospect research from the library's internal records. Should patrons' records be part of the prospect research tool kit or not? Internal donor records are usually included in prospect research, as is any information gathered by your library director or fundraisers through meetings and interactions with prospects and donors. How will your library director and fundraisers share this information with the librarians doing prospect research? Will all the information be shared, or just the information that the library director or fundraisers determine is relevant to prospect research? These are all questions to consider for the confidentiality policy.

Who Has Access to Prospect Research

The confidentiality policy must specify who has access to prospect research profiles and who will write them. This should be a small group of staff who either will be doing the research or will be meeting with donors and prospects. One of the key components of the policy—and the reason the policy is signed by staff—is that it will specify under which circumstances information is shared and with whom. More important, it will stipulate that prospect research information is not shared in any way whatsoever with others not specifically mentioned in the policy. The policy should also specify whether or not library volunteers or trustees will have access to research profiles or a redacted version of them, perhaps with all the wealth information and the giving amounts to the library removed. You must be certain that this policy does not violate any existing library policies. There also should be a compelling reason to share such information with library volunteers. If you define what those situations would be, then include that option in the policy to allow for the rare occasion when your library director needs it. Any volunteers who might have access to research profiles will also have to sign and be bound by the confidentiality policy.

Storing Research Profiles and Worksheets

If your library has a donor database, then you will probably store research profiles in it, within the prospects' records. Make sure that your policy is in accordance with those policies that determine who have access to the donor database. It is important to be restrictive about who has access to research profiles. If it is not possible to allow different levels of access to the donor database or if you do not have a donor database, store your research profiles and worksheets on a secure network drive with limited staff access or on a password-controlled individual computer so that there is restricted, controlled access to this information. Be sure to provide guidelines in your confidentiality policy on where the electronic versions of the research profiles and research worksheets are stored.

The confidentiality policy should specify that staff should not forward research profiles or worksheets via e-mail unless you can encrypt the information. E-mail is not a secure method for transmission, and there is always the possibility of accidently forwarding research profiles or worksheets to the wrong person.

The policy should also cover the storage of paper files, such as research worksheets and any other backup documentation gathered during prospect research, such as property records, SEC filings, or news articles, to name just a few examples. These files also must be in a locked, secure area with restricted

access. Include in the confidentiality policy that any documents no longer needed should be shredded immediately.

Writing a Confidentiality Policy

If your institution is large enough to have a legal department, seek their help in
putting the policy together. If your library has a lawyer on the advisory board,
perhaps he or she can assist your library with writing the policy. If not, then try
searching for examples of other prospect research departments' confidentiality
policies on the Internet, using the search terms "*confidentiality policy*" and "*prospect
research*" or something similar. Contact those research departments and ask for
permission to base your policy on theirs.

Ethical Standards and the Donor Bill of Rights

APRA is the professional organization for prospect research; it is a good idea to
be familiar with their "Statement of Ethics" policy, which provides guidelines
for the basic standards under which prospect research should be conducted (box
2.1). This is included at the end of this chapter along with the "Donor Bill of
Rights," which address what the donor should expect from a nonprofit organization (box 2.2). The "Donor Bill of Rights" was developed by the American
Association of Fund Raising Counsel (AAFRC); the Association of Fund Raising Professionals (AFP); the Association for Healthcare Philanthropy (AHP); and
the Council for Advancement and Support of Education (CASE), and is endorsed
by APRA International.

BOX 2.1

APRA'S STATEMENT OF ETHICS

In 2008 the APRA board charged the Ethics Committee to prepare an updated revision
of APRA's Statement of Ethics, focusing on the broad essentials of ethics rather than
the details of our day-to-day work. In response, the committee reviewed the code of
ethics of many fundraising associations and research organizations and drafted a new
statement that focused on what committee members considered to the four essentials
of ethical conduct: personal integrity, accountability, practice, and conflict of interest.
The board approved the statement in December 2008.

Any reproduction of the APRA Ethics Statement must include recognition of APRA.

APRA members shall support and further the individual's fundamental right to
privacy and protect the confidential information of their institutions. APRA members
are committed to the ethical collection and use of information. Members shall follow
all applicable national, state, and local laws, as well as institutional policies, governing
the collection, use, maintenance, and dissemination of information in the pursuit of the
missions of their institutions.

CODE OF ETHICS

Advancement researchers must balance an individual's right to privacy with the needs of their institutions to collect, analyze, record, maintain, use, and disseminate information. This balance is not always easy to maintain. To guide researchers, the following ethical principles apply:

Preamble

Establishing and maintaining ethical and professional standards is a primary goal of the mission of the Association of Professional Researchers for Advancement (APRA). All APRA members shall support and further an individual's fundamental right to privacy and protect the confidential information of their institutions. All members agree to abide by this Statement of Ethics in the daily conduct of all professional activity encompassing the gathering, dissemination, and use of information for the purposes of fundraising or other institutional advancement activity.

Four fundamental principles provide the foundation for the ethical conduct of fundraising research, relationship management, and analytics: integrity, accountability, practice, and conflict of interest.

Integrity

Members shall be truthful with respect to their identities and purpose and the identity of their institutions during the course of their work. They shall continually strive to increase the recognition and respect of the profession.

Accountability

Members shall respect the privacy of donors and prospects and conduct their work with the highest level of discretion. They shall adhere to the spirit as well as the letter of all applicable laws and all policies of their organization. They shall conduct themselves in the utmost professional manner in accordance with the standards of their organization.

Practice

Members shall take the necessary care to ensure that their work is as accurate as possible. They shall only record data that is appropriate to the fundraising process and protect the confidentiality of all personal information at all times.

Conflicts of Interest

Members shall avoid competing professional or personal interests and shall disclose such interests to their institutions at the first instance. A conflict of interest can create an appearance of impropriety that can undermine confidence in the member, their organization, and the profession.

BOX 2.2

DONOR BILL OF RIGHTS

Philanthropy is based on voluntary action for the common good. It is a tradition of giving and sharing that is primary to the quality of life. To assure that philanthropy merits the respect and trust of the general public, and that donors and prospective donors can have full confidence in the not-for-profit organizations and causes they are asked to support, we declare that all donors have these rights:

- To be informed of the organization's mission, of the way the organization intends to use donated resources, and of its capacity to use donations effectively for their intended purposes.
- To be informed of the identity of those serving on the organization's governing board, and to expect the board to exercise prudent judgment in its stewardship responsibilities.
- To have access to the organization's most recent financial statements.
- To be assured their gifts will be used for the purposes for which they were given.
- To receive appropriate acknowledgment and recognition.
- To be assured that information about their donations is handled with respect and with confidentiality to the extent provided by law.
- To expect that all relationships with individuals representing organizations of interest to the donor will be professional in nature.
- To be informed whether those seeking donations are volunteers, employees of the organization or hired solicitors.
- To have the opportunity for their names to be deleted from mailing lists that an organization may intend to share.
- To feel free to ask questions when making a donation and to receive prompt, truthful and forthright answers.

DEVELOPED BY

- American Association of Fund Raising Counsel (AAFRC)
- Association of Fund Raising Professionals (AFP)
- Association for Healthcare Philanthropy (AHP)
- Council for Advancement and Support of Education (CASE)

ENDORSED BY

- Independent Sector
- National Catholic Development Conference (NCDC)
- National Committee on Planned Giving (NCPG)
- National Council for Resource Development (NCRD)
- United Way of America

Source: APRA, www.aprahome.org/p/cm/ld/fid=115.

Biographical
Information

BIOGRAPHICAL INFORMATION IS personal information about your prospects, such as their age; where they live, work, and went to school; and information about their family members. It is essential to have good background biographical information about your prospects. This is critical for a number of reasons. Firstly, you need biographical information in order to begin researching wealth indicators about the prospect. For example, once you know the home address for a prospect, then you can find a value for their home. Secondly, biographical information provides a good basis for both the library director or fundraising staff to build a relationship with the prospect. If your fundraising staff is going to ask a prospect for a donation, it helps to know about him or her. Thirdly, it helps establish that your information is consistent for each prospect. Much like authority control in library cataloging, you need to know that the biographical information you find and provide in a research profile for your prospect, John Smith, is consistent for all research profiles. Gathering personal information about your prospects is the first step in working on prospect research. The information that you find will be used to start writing a research profile on your prospect.

Prospects Affiliated with Your Library
You already have library patrons who are prospects. For the prospects who are affiliated with your library, you should have their names and addresses, either through library records or

giving records for gifts made to your library. You may also have other information about them, such as their current employers and their families, including their spouse's/partner's name. The fundraising staff or the library director may also be able to provide information about family relationships for prospects they know. If your library director or fundraiser knows the prospect and can fill in details about his or her employment history, education, or family information, then getting this information is a good first step. After you get this "inside" information, the next step is verifying it, if possible or necessary.

Basic Biographical Information

When you begin your research, it's best to start by writing down everything that you know about the prospect. Continue filling in information as you find it. A template is provided in this chapter; you should adapt the worksheet template to fit your research needs. Each piece of information you find will give you a direction for finding the next piece of the puzzle about your prospect. Ideally you will be able to find your prospect's age, current employer, job title, employment history, and education. You should look for this same information for your prospect's spouse/partner. It is also useful to try to find the prospect's parents' names, ages, and background, as well as the parents of your prospect's spouse/partner. Information about parents is especially important if it will impact the relationship with the prospect, or if it will make a difference in determining their wealth. (For example, if your prospect is the son of Warren Buffett, it would be useful to know this.) Unfortunately, this information is often very hard to find, and you will not always be able to find all this information or even most of it for each prospect. Nevertheless, it is worthwhile to try.

There are some subscription databases that compile background information on a prospect for you; with one search you can find property, employment, giving, and much more. WealthEngine (www.wealthengine.com), for example, compiles information on prospects using multiple sources. WealthEngine's search is by personal name and home address, and may return information about employment, stock holdings, nonprofit and political gifts, property holdings, and family foundations. However, such database subscriptions can be expensive.

Verifying Information

Throughout your search it is critical to verify that you have found information on your prospect and not someone who has the same name. This should always be in the forefront of your mind while conducting your research. Once you start doing prospect research, you will be very surprised to learn how common seemingly uncommon names actually are. A name that seems entirely unique is very likely not unique; there could even be more than one person with that name living in the same city, such as a father and son or two unrelated people with the same name. More common names can be even trickier, as it is possible that there are two related or unrelated people with the same name working in the same industry or the same company.

To verify that the new information you find is regarding the "correct" person, fact-check the new information with the information that you already know about the prospect, such as the age of your prospect, work history, education, or spouse's/partner's name. The researcher often must rely on his logic and critical thinking skills. For example, if you know that your prospect graduated from the University of Michigan with a BA in English in 1990, and then you find information about someone with your prospect's name who earned an MBA from the University of Chicago in 1988, you can deduce that the MBA was not earned by your prospect. Because it is unlikely that your prospect earned a graduate degree before earning an undergraduate degree, or that they went back to school to earn a second bachelor's degree after earning an MBA. However if the graduation dates were reversed, you would want to keep the information about the MBA until you are either able to confirm that it is your prospect (or a close relative of your prospect) or that it isn't.

Sometimes it isn't possible to confirm information you find is about your prospect. If this happens, you can make a note of the information and ask your fundraising staff or library director about it. If the pertinent information comes up in a later conversation with the prospect and your fundraising staff knows that you need that information, they can find it out and pass it on to you. It is just as important to let the library director or fundraising staff know the information that you cannot find and verify on your prospect as it is to let them know what you have been able to find or confirm. Through the relationship with the prospect, they might be able to fill in the gaps, which will give you a more complete picture of your prospect.

Personal Bios on Company Websites

The first place to start when researching a prospect is on their employer's website. Sometimes you will get lucky in finding biographical information that has been compiled for you. If your prospect works at a company that provides such information online, then you will be able to find a great deal of information in one place, such as employment history, education and civic affiliations, and more. Another advantage to this is that you can be fairly sure that the information is accurate, as the information is likely to have been provided for the company bio by the prospect himself or herself. So, if you know where your prospect works, be sure to consult this resource first.

Discovering the Prospect's Employer

Sometimes you might know where your prospect lives, but not where they work. In this case a free source to try is the Federal Election Commission's transaction query (www.fec.gov/finance/disclosure/norindsea.shtml), which lists public information on political donations of $200 or more. Use the advanced donor search for your prospect's name, limited by the state or city where your prospect lives. The results will be displayed and show the amount of the gift, year, and candidate or PAC. There will also be a link to the filing of the gift through the Federal Election Commission (FEC) that includes the prospect's employer. This method works well for finding a spouse's/partner's employment information too. However, unless your prospect has made a political donation of $200 or more, they will not be listed. (You should also include the political donation in the research profile; political donations are covered in chapter 8.)

Background on the Employer

It is also helpful to provide some background in your prospect's research profile on the company where they work. Review the company's website to find out what kind of company it is. Check to see if your prospect's family owns the company, and whether it is a private or a public company. Some of this information will be listed on the company website or found through the subscription based databases of Hoover's (www.hoovers.com) or Dun and Bradstreet (www.dandb.com) or any other source that provides information about companies and is available to you through your library's reference collections. These sources may also list ownership information about the company and most recent annual sales. (Finding stock holdings and compensation information for an executive in a public company are covered in chapter 6.)

Employment History and Education

When you have found where your prospect works or if you know where he or she went to school, you should have enough information to search the free resource LinkedIn (www.linkedin.com), which usually provides employment information, employment history, and education. The information in LinkedIn profiles is entered by the individual, so you can usually rely on the accuracy of it.

Some LinkedIn profiles can't be viewed unless you or your library has a LinkedIn profile. Security setting preferences should be discussed with your library director. Through LinkedIn, you can set your privacy settings so that either the prospect can or cannot see that you looked at his or her LinkedIn profile. As mentioned above, when using LinkedIn you will need to know some basic information about your prospect in order to be sure you have found the right profile. Per LinkedIn's website, there are more than two hundred million registered users, so it is key to be sure you are looking at the profile of your prospect.

News Sources

It is useful to search the Internet with the search terms of your prospect's name and the company name where he or she works or any other relevant search terms, such as the city where your prospect lives. Also try news searches with these search terms, using Proquest (www.proquest.com), Factiva (www.dowjones.com/factiva), or your preferred database news sources. When you find your prospect's parents' names (and the parents' names of the spouse/partner), then try finding news articles on them using the same methods described above.

Wedding Announcements and Obituaries

When you search on your prospect's name and your prospect's spouse's/partner's name (and parents' names and children's names), you may come across wedding announcements for your prospect's adult children or obituaries for family members. Both of these are extremely good sources for finding family information, which can be some of the most difficult information to track down through public sources.

Wedding announcements and obituaries can be found through news searches. There is a subscription service for obituaries that is very useful to consult, Obituary Data.com (www.obituarydata.com). You will need the name of the deceased to search this site. The Social Security Death Index, which is provided for free through Ancestry.com (www.ancestry.com) and other sources, will give you a date of death for an individual who died three or more years ago. As of 2014, new privacy laws restrict access to death information through the Social Security Death Index for individuals who died within three years in order to protect access to social security numbers. If a published obituary exists, then you will be able to find death information on your prospect's relatives.

Birth Dates and Ages

The birth date and age of your prospect, your prospect's spouse/partner, and family members are often challenging to find. If your prospect is on the board or is an executive of a public company, then his or her age might be listed on documents filed with the US Securities and Exchange Commission (described in detail in chapter 6). You also will be able to find the birth month and year through subscription-based LexisNexis (see below) for your prospect, and your prospect's spouse/partner, and possibly any parents as well. Wedding announcements and obituaries sometimes provide ages, and you can also deduce ages by graduation years for your prospect or your prospect's family members.

Prospects' Spouses and Partners

It is important to get the name of a prospect's spouse/partner if you can. Verifying a spouse's/partner's name can be done through the subscription-based Lexis-

Nexis for Development Professionals (www.lexisnexis.com/en-us/products/ln
-development-professionals.page) by consulting property ownership records for
your prospect or reviewing property records found through the county assessor's
office. (How to find property records is covered in chapter 4.)

LexisNexis provides personal information on individuals, such as the month
and year an individual was born and family members' names and ages. However, family members are not identified by relationships. LexisNexis identifies
people as relatives, but which ones are the siblings, spouses, in-laws, parents and
children is not stated; only the names and ages are provided. Nevertheless, you
might be able to deduce who the parents and children are based on their names
and ages.

Maiden Names

Finding the maiden name of a wife when she has taken her husband's name can
be challenging. She may use her maiden name as part of her name, either as a
middle name or a hyphenated last name. Also be sure to check whether she is
using a married name from a previous marriage; an obituary for her mother or
father or a wedding announcement for the prospect can help provide this information. Another option is to find her maiden name through donations she has
made to her college or high school. You can find donations through the subscription-based NOZA (https://www.nozasearch.com), which will often list the gift
with the class year and include the maiden name, as well as the spouse's name,
so you know you have the "correct" person. Of course, men may take their
spouse's/partner's names or combine names or change their names. A Lexis-
Nexis search may also provide all the forms of the prospect's and the spouse's/
partner's names.

Parents

Information on parents is not absolutely critical, but it is useful if it indicates
something about the prospect's wealth or has an impact on the relationship with
the prospect. You should try to find the names, ages, and backgrounds of your
prospect's parents and your prospect's spouse's/partner's parents. Once you have
these names and ages, try searching using the same methods used for your prospect to find more information on them.

It is also useful to know if your prospect's parents and in-laws are living. If your library director is having lunch with a prospect and their parent
recently died, it could be awkward to go to that meeting without knowing
this information.

Family Trees and Genealogical Information

Ancestry.com (www.ancestry.com) is fee-based and a good source to find family
information about your prospect, especially if he or she is related to or could be

related to a prominent family (rich or famous). A general Internet search may also confirm whether your prospect is related to a prominent family. It is easy to get carried away with genealogy research, so keep in mind that you do not need to track the prospect's line back to the *Mayflower*; just check to see if they are directly related to a prominent family.

Social Media Sources

Social media sources are useful in determining family relationships and personal interests of prospects. However, they must be used with caution. While you are working on the policies for your library for prospect research, it is important to consider how you will use social media websites and even whether or not you will use Facebook or any other social media websites as a source for research. Such websites, especially Facebook, can be an excellent source for figuring out family relationships. Access to Facebook (www.facebook.com) is free, but you will need to set up an account to use it.

There will be some prospects who have a very large presence on the Internet and write blogs; have Twitter (https://twitter.com) accounts, Pinterest (http://pinterest.com) profiles, or Foursquare (https://foursquare.com), Flickr (www.flickr.com), or YouTube (www.youtube.com) accounts; or participate in any other social media websites. It is very easy to get lost in the sheer volume of information. So, it is key to consider that the purpose of collecting biographical information is not to record absolutely everything about a prospect, but to build a picture of the prospect's background with the goal of turning the prospect into a donor to your library. With that in mind, determine what is relevant information and what is not. Use these social media websites based on your library director's policy about them and fill in the research profile with all the information you are able to find that is relevant. You may wish to list the social media websites that your prospect participates in, in case your fundraisers or library director would like to review them.

The Research Profile

In the biographical section of the research profile, include the full name of the prospect, the spouse's/partner's full name and maiden name if you can find it, and their ages and birth dates. Include employment information for the prospect and the prospect's spouse/partner, and provide background information about the company as well. Also include where they went to school, the degrees earned, and graduation years, if you can find any of this. Include information about the prospect's adult children, if that information is available, and any adult children of his or her spouse/partner. The prospect's parents' and spouse's/partner's parents' names and ages, and any background information about them, should also be included if you can find it.

PRACTICE EXAMPLE 1

You are researching a prospect, but you only have their name and the home address. You need to find where they work.

- Because the name is uncommon, you try a general Internet search and news searches with the person's name and the hometown as search terms. When you get results, you verify that the employment information is on your prospect and not someone with your prospect's name by fact-checking the new information against the information that you already have.
- You also search for your prospect on the Federal Election Commission (FEC) website (www.fec.gov/finance/disclosure/norindsea.shtml). Your prospect has made a political donation of over $200, so the results list both the home address of your prospect and your prospect's employer.
- You decided to check a second prospect and were not able to find or verify the employment information. You notified your fundraising staff; hopefully they will be able to get this information for you as a relationship develops between the prospect and the library director or fundraisers.

PRACTICE EXAMPLE 2

Your fundraiser tells you that a prospect is part of the Rockefeller family. You need to verify this for your library director.

- You ask your fundraiser how this information was obtained. The prospect mentioned this to the fundraiser, but it still needs to be verified at least to determine what this may mean about your prospect's wealth. (If the only information the fundraiser has is that the prospect's last name is Rockefeller, you will have to do some research. However, it's useful to know if the fundraiser did not get this information from the prospect.)
- You find a history of the Rockefeller family and a family tree through Ancestry.com (www.ancestry.com) or other genealogy resources available to you. You find that there is a lot of documentation on the direct descendants of John D. Rockefeller Sr. You determine whether that your prospect is a direct descendant rather quickly.

PRACTICE EXAMPLE 3

You have your prospect's married name and would like to find her maiden name.

- A quick search on LexisNexis (www.lexisnexis.com/en-us/products/ln -development-professionals.page) provides all the names used by by your prospect. The list of relatives, which includes names and ages, also gives you clues about the prospect's maiden name.

- You search through news sources for a wedding announcement or obituaries using her first name and her spouse's name as search terms.
- Another option is searching in subscription-based NOZA (https://www .nozasearch.com) using the prospect's name. You find a gift made to a high school listing the prospect's maiden name and graduation year in the gift information.
- Your fundraiser points out that asking the prospect about her maiden name may not be the best idea, if you could not find it through the suggestions listed above. This could be an awkward question. It might be better to ask about her high school or college degree, and hopefully that information could lead to the discovery of the prospect's maiden name.

ONLINE SOURCES

Fee-based

Ancestry.com .... www.ancestry.com
Provides genealogy information, family trees and information on family backgrounds.

Dun and Bradstreet .... www.dandb.com
Provides information about the company where your prospect works and may also provide information about the ownership of the company.

Factiva .... www.dowjones.com/factiva
Gives access to news sources and journals. You can search a prospect's name and other search terms for news articles on your prospect.

Hoover's .... www.hoovers.com
Provides information about the company where your prospect works and may also provide biographical information on your prospect.

LexisNexis .... www.lexisnexis.com/
en-us/products/ln-development-professionals.page
Provides biographical information on a prospect, including the birth month and year, relatives' names, and the forms of a personal name of the prospect or the prospect's spouse. It also provides property records for most properties in the United States; those records may include a prospect's spouse's name as well.

Obituary Data.com .... www.obituarydata.com
Provides obituaries, which include the names of immediately family members.

NOZA .... https://www.nozasearch.com
Gives information about gifts made to nonprofits by your prospect or your prospect's spouse/partner and may provide information about a maiden name (look for gifts made to a college or high school).

Proquest .... www.proquest.com
Provides news searches to find information about your prospect's background and family information.

WealthEngine .... www.wealthengine.com
Compiles information on prospects when the personal name and home address are known. The results may include employment information, stock holdings, nonprofit and political gifts, property holdings, and family foundations.

Free

LinkedIn .... www.linkedin.com
Provides profiles on individuals, which may include their current employer, past employment history, and education.

FEC Transaction Query...www.fec.gov/
finance/disclosure/norindsea.shtml
Provides information on individuals who have made a political donation of $200 or more. The gift amount, year, candidate or PAC who received the gift, home address, and employment information on the donor is listed. This is useful to find current or past employment information for the prospect or the prospect's spouse/partner.

Social Security Death Index
Accessed through Ancestry.com .... www.ancestry.com
Provides death dates for deceased relatives of your prospect, who died three years ago or more.

Free Social Media Sites

Facebook .... www.facebook.com
May provide family relationships, education or current employer, as well as interests.

Foursquare .... https://foursquare.com
Shows which restaurants and shops and activities your prospect likes.

Pinterest .... http://pinterest.com
Allows users to post images from and links to other websites, based on themes,

that are of interest to them, such as cooking, fashion, or decorating; will show interests of the prospect.

Twitter .... **https://twitter.com**
May provide employer information and show interests of the prospect.

YouTube .... **www.youtube.com**
May provide videos on your prospect, including interviews.

BIOGRAPHICAL RESEARCH WORKSHEET TEMPLATE

CONFIDENTIAL

Researcher's name: Date:

PROSPECT

NAME:

Maiden name:

Source(s):

Notes:

BIRTH DATE:

Source(s):

Notes:

HOME ADDRESS:

Source(s):

Notes:

CURRENT EMPLOYER:

Title: Start date:

Company information (private or public):

Type of business:

Annual sales: $

Source(s):

Notes:

PAST EMPLOYERS

1. Employer's name:

  Title: Dates employed:

2. Employer's Name:

  Title: Dates employed:

3. Employer's name:

  Title: Dates employed:

Source(s):

Notes:

EDUCATION

1. School:

  Degree: Graduation date:

2. School:

  Degree: Graduation date:

Source(s):

Notes:

PROSPECT'S SPOUSE/PARTNER

NAME:

Maiden name:

Source(s):

Notes:

BIRTH DATE:

Source(s):

Notes:

WEDDING DATE:

Source(s):

Notes:

CURRENT EMPLOYER:

Title: Start date:

Company information (private or public):

Type of business:

Annual sales: $

Source(s):

Notes:

PAST EMPLOYER

Employer's name:

Title: Dates employed:

Source(s):

Notes:

EDUCATION

1. School:

   Degree: Graduation date:

2. School:

   Degree: Graduation date:

Source(s):

Notes:

PROSPECT'S ADULT CHILDREN

NAME: Birth date:

Home address:

Education:

Current employer:

Source(s):

Notes:

NAME: Birth date:

Home address:

Education:

Current employer:

Source(s):

Notes:

NAME: Birth date:

Home address:

Education:

Current employer:

Source(s):

Notes:

PROSPECT'S PARENTS AND IN-LAWS

FATHER'S NAME:

Birth date (and/or death date):

Home address:

Education:

Employer:

Other family information:

Source(s):

Notes:

MOTHER'S NAME:

Birth date (and/or death date):

Maiden name:

Home address:

Education:

Employer:

Other family information:

Source(s):

Notes:

FATHER-IN-LAW'S NAME:

Birth date (and/or death date):

Home address:

Education:

Employer:

Other family information:

Source(s):

Notes:

MOTHER-IN-LAW'S NAME:

Birth date (and/or death date):

Maiden name:

Home address:

Education:

Employer:

Other family information:

Source(s):

Notes:

Real Estate

REAL ESTATE IS one of the most available indicators of wealth that you can find for a prospect, and it is often the only wealth indicator that you will be able to find. This makes real estate particularly useful. Also, it is an excellent benchmark to compare and rank the prospects in your prospect pool. For instance, if you find that the prospect you are researching owns a $3 million home, then you will be able to identify him or her as more able to give a major gift to your library than a prospect who owns a condominium worth $100,000. Of course, this may not be the case, but remember: you are not trying to predict the future, only coming up with a best guess.

County Assessors

If you know addresses for your prospect, you can find information about home ownership and other real estate ownership by consulting property records. In the United States, property records are publicly available through the county assessor's office for the county where the property is located. So, the first step is using the home address for your prospect to determine which county your prospect's home is located. Once you have this information, then you can begin tracking down the property record for the home and finding its approximate value.

Start by checking to see if that county has a website by using the Tax Assessor Database (www.pulawski.net); this information is organized by state. Not all county assessors' offices make property records available online or for free, but many do. For some counties you can also call to verify property ownership over the telephone for free. When searching for property records online within a county assessors' website, in most cases, you will need to know the address of the property. You should search by address, the name of your prospect, or the name of the spouse/partner to find the record. How to access the records varies county by county; however, after searching for a few property records from different counties or states, you will get the feel for how to do it pretty quickly. Also keep in mind that if a property was purchased very recently, it may take time for the record to show up in the county's database.

Additionally, searching for property records through a county assessor's office will give you information on the address that you have for your prospect—it will not give you all of the prospect's property holdings, if those properties are located in a different county or a different state.

Finding All Property Holdings

Some versions of the subscription-based LexisNexis, including LexisNexis for Development Professionals, provides access to property records and lists all properties owned under the prospect's name. Through LexisNexis, you can find all property holdings for an individual, including vacation homes in a different state from their primary residence. If your library has a subscription to LexisNexis, then it may provide this access; if not, it might be worthwhile getting this subscription for one or some of the librarians in your library. Property records for all properties owned by a prospect are also available through the subscription-based iWave Information Systems (iwave.com/prospect-research-online).

If your library does not have the budget to purchase a database to find property records, you can assume that the prospect you are researching owns their home, if the county assessor's office does not provide this information for free. You can use any number of websites to get an estimate for the market value of a property, such as Zillow (www.zillow.com) or Yahoo! Homes (http://homes .yahoo.com/home-worth).

Property Records

What is contained in the property record, available through a county assessor's office, varies from county to county. For instance, Cook County in Illinois does not list the owner's name. Most property records include the owner's name; a brief description of the property, including the address; the purchase price of the property; and the property index number (PIN), also referred to as the parcel number, which is a unique number assigned to a property. The property records available through both iWave and LexisNexis include all the information listed above and may also include information about the mortgage. These records are also useful for finding out the sales price for a property previously owned by your prospect.

Fair Market Value

The property record may also include some value of the property as well, which might be the assessed value or the fair market value. The definition of fair market value is "the price of a home that a buyer and a seller agree upon to the best of their ability and their own personal interests. For example, if a son buys a property from his mother at an unusually low price, that price isn't the fair market value because the mom acted in her son's interests rather than in the strict economic definition of her own personal interests."[1] This is the price a seller would expect to get for his or her home.

Assessed Value

The assessed value of real estate property is used to calculate property taxes: "the value placed on a property by the town or city's assessor's office for the purpose of determining the property tax due."[2] The assessed value is often lower than the market value.

Finding Values for Real Estate

The purpose of using real estate when researching a prospect is to try, with the limited information that is available, to flag prospects as potential major gift donors for the fundraisers or the director to direct their focus. Include a value for the property in the research profile. It is best to use the estimated market value, found through Yahoo! Homes, Zillow, or a similar website. You can also use the fair market value for the home listed on the property record. Because the assessed value tends to be a lower value, you shouldn't use it unless you can't find the estimated market value or the fair market value.

Mortgages

Many people do not own their home outright and take out a loan to purchase their property. That loan is a mortgage. Property records may also include information about a mortgage that is on the property. There are different types of mortgages that are based on the interest rate of the loan and the length of the repayment schedule. The two most common types of mortgages are repaid over fifteen years or over thirty years and have an interest rate that either does not change, which is called a fixed rate, or has an interest rate that does change, which is called an adjustable rate.

Some property records include the basic terms of a mortgage, such as the purchase price and type of the mortgage. On a property record you will not be able to find the full terms of the mortgage. If the sale price of the home, the mortgage amount, and the interest rate are listed on the property record, then you may wish to include this information in your research on your prospect. You can assume that the down payment on the home is the difference between the mortgage amount and the sale price of the home.

Mortgage Calculators

You can use a mortgage calculator to get an estimate for the monthly house payments for the home. The mortgage calculator offered through CNN Money (http://cgi.money.cnn.com/tools/mortgagecalc) includes estimates for property taxes and real estate insurance, which are part of the house payment but are not included in the property record. Plug in the purchase price, the down payment, and other mortgage information listed on the property record to get an estimate of the monthly house payment.

Real estate values and interest rates on mortgages have varied wildly over the past decade, so if you find a property record for a home that was purchased several years ago, you may wish to use a mortgage calculator that allows more information to be included, such as the calculator found at www.mortgagecalculator.org.

Underwater Mortgages

Sometimes the amount owed on a mortgage is more than the current value of the home. This is called an underwater or upside-down mortgage. You cannot determine with certainty that the prospect you are researching has a mortgage that is underwater, because you will not have an actual appraisal value for the home—just a rough value from Zillow or another website or the market value estimated by the county assessor's office. Another issue to consider is that the mortgage may have been refinanced, and there will not necessarily be a property record showing the new terms of the mortgage.

The problem with an upside-down or underwater mortgage is that selling the home will not pay off the mortgage. So, if the prospect is planning to sell his or her house, an underwater mortgage could potentially be a problem that may have an impact on the prospect making a gift. If the prospect is not planning to sell the home, then it isn't an issue, of course, as the value of the home may recover.

Because you will never know the full economic picture for your prospect, it is not necessary to focus too closely on the details of the estimated value of the home in comparison to the mortgage owed. You will not actually be able to verify either piece of information, and trying to do so does not add value to the research on your prospect.

Foreclosures

If you discover that your prospect's home is in foreclosure, that is a sign of financial difficulties that might impact the prospect's potential to make a gift to your library. As Redfin defines it, "Foreclosure is a process that transfers the right of home ownership from the homeowner to the bank or lender. A home goes into foreclosure when the owner defaults on his mortgage loan payments."[3] If the prospect you are researching is having financial difficulties, your fundraising staff or library director should decide whether or not to pursue the prospect for a gift.

Trusts

If the property record is held by a trust, you should not assume that your prospect owns the property. You may wish to make an exception if the trust includes the prospect's name or the spouse's/partner's name; for example, the John Smith Trust. However, you will not be able to find the terms of the trust, so it is an assumption that the property is fully owned by your prospect. If a property is owned by a trust, it's a judgment call whether to use the value of the property or not. If the property is held in someone else's name from your prospect or your prospect's spouse/partner, then your prospect could be renting the property.

Co-ops

If the property is a cooperative (co-op) and not a condominium, there will not be property records for the individual units. According to the National Association of Housing Cooperatives, "Cooperative members own a share in a corporation that owns or controls the building(s) and/or property in which they live. Each shareholder is entitled to occupy a specific unit and has a vote in the corporation. Every month, shareholders pay an amount that covers their proportionate share of the expense of operating the entire cooperative, which typically includes underlying mortgage payments, property taxes, management, maintenance, insurance, utilities, and contributions to reserve funds."[4] If you are not able to find a property record for a property, search for the building address in Google to determine whether the property is a co-op. If your property is not in one of the five boroughs of New York City, there will not be publicly available property records for units in co-op buildings, so you will not be able to determine the actually market value for your prospect's unit in the building. However, you may be able to find a unit that is for sale in the building, which will give you an approximate value for the unit you are researching.

The exception to this is if the co-op is located in New York City. There is a searchable, free database (ACRIS, http://a836-acris.nyc.gov/DS) that provides property records and is searchable by address, parcel number, or owner's name. The results list includes a link to an image, which is how the property record is displayed.

Wealthy Zip Codes

Forbes publishes an annual list of the most expensive zip codes in the United States (see, for example, the 2012 report, www.forbes.com/special-report/2012/1016 _zip-codes.html). This is a good source to use for sorting through a large list of prospects; you can compare the zip codes of your prospects to the *Forbes* zip codes list. Start by researching the prospects who live within the zip codes identified by *Forbes*, because they are likely to be the wealthiest people in your prospect pool.

The Research Profile

The research profile for your prospect should include all the properties owned by your prospect or your prospect's spouse/partner, including the full address and the market value of each piece of property. If you have the basic terms of the mortgage and the down payment for each property, you may wish to include that information as well. If your prospect recently sold a property, that information is also helpful to include, especially the sales price of the home and the date it was sold.

PRACTICE EXAMPLE 1

You have the home address of your prospect, and your library director would like to know the market value of the prospect's home.

- You verify that your prospect owns his home by finding the property records by using your subscription to LexisNexis or iWave, searching for property under the prospect's name and the prospect's spouse's name. This gives you both the property record for the prospect's home and property records for any other homes that the prospect owns, including a vacation home in another state.
- You use Zillow or another website to find the market values for the home or homes.
- Another option would be to search the county assessor's website for the county where the property is located. Use Zillow or another website to find the market value for the home, if that figure is not listed on the property record.
- If there is no access to property records through the county assessor, or if access costs money and it isn't in the library budget to cover that cost, then it is possible to assume your prospect owns his home and use Zillow or another website to find the market value for the home.

PRACTICE EXAMPLE 2

You are having difficulty finding a property record for the prospect you are researching, and your fundraising staff would like you to verify that the prospect owns her home.

- Search the county assessor's office, LexisNexis, or iWave for the property by address, by the prospect's name, and the prospect's spouse's name. (If you find the property and it is listed under someone else's name, then your prospect may be renting the property.)
- You are still unable to find the property, so you verify that the property records are available online and for free by looking at the county assessor's website. (You can also use LexisNexis or iWave by checking to see that the county is included in the property records.)
- Property records in general are available through the source you are using, and the property is a unit in a building. You check to see if the building is a co-operative, which it is. You find a current listing for a unit that is for sale in the building or a recent sale of a unit, and you use that as a rough value for the unit that your prospect lives in.

ONLINE SOURCES

Fee-based

iWave Information Systems .... iwave.com/prospect-research-online
Provides property records, which are searchable by address and owner's name.

LexisNexis .... www.lexisnexis.com
Provides property records for most properties in the United States. A feature in LexisNexis provides a list for you of all the properties associated with your prospect. Because you can search for property records by the owner's name, seller's name, or property address, you should be able to find most property records using these searchers.

Free

ACRIS http://a836-acris.nyc.gov/DS
Provides property records for units in co-op buildings in New York City. The database is searchable by address, parcel number, or owner's name. From the results list, select the image to display the property record.

Tax Assessor Database .... www.pulawski.net
Provides links to county assessor's websites; through those sites, property records may be available.

Yahoo! Homes ....http://homes.yahoo.com/home-worth
Searchable by address and provides you with a market value for the home.

Zillow .... www.zillow.com
Provides the same information as Yahoo! Homes, but may also include a photograph
and the most recent sales price of the home.

Mortgage Calculator .... www.mortgagecalculator.org
Allows you to calculate the mortgage payment starting with a past date. This is
useful for homes purchased several years ago. It will give you an estimate of the
amount still owed on the mortgage.

CNN Money Mortgage Calculator .... http://cgi.money.cnn.com/
tools/mortgagecalc
Provides a quick way to calculate an estimate for a monthly house payment when
you have the sales price of the home and the mortgage amount from a property
record.

Forbes **Wealthiest Zip Codes** .... www.forbes.com/
special-report/2012/1016_zip-codes.html
Lists the highest home values in the United States; produced annually. This list
is useful to use as a starting point if you have a very large, unexamined prospect
pool. Search to see which of your prospects live in the wealthiest zip codes and
start researching that group first.

NOTES
1. "Fair Market Value," Redfin, last modified January 7, 2011,
   www.redfin.com/definition/fair-market-value.
2. "Assessed vs. Appraisal Values," Zillow, accessed March 20, 2013,
   www.zillow.com/wikipages/Assessed-Values-vs-Appraised-Values.
3. "Foreclosure Definition," Redfin, last modified May 23, 2011,
   www.redfin.com/definition/foreclosure.
4. "What Is a Housing Cooperative?" National Association of Housing Cooperatives,
   accessed March 24, 2013, www.coophousing.org/DisplayPage.aspx?id=48.

REAL ESTATE HOLDINGS RESEARCH WORKSHEET TEMPLATE

CONFIDENTIAL

PROSPECT'S NAME:

Researcher's name: Date:

REAL ESTATE HOLDINGS

PROPERTY #1

Street address:

City, state, zip code:

Owned by (name(s) on property record):

Type of residence: primary residence   vacation home

Purchase price: $

Purchase date:

Current value of property: $

Type of value: market   assessed

Source(s):

Property record attached or saved electronically: yes   no

Notes:

PROPERTY #2

Street address:

City, state, zip code:

Owned by:

Type of residence: primary residence   vacation home

Purchase price: $

Purchase date:

Current value of property: $

Type of value: market   assessed

Source(s):

Property record attached or saved electronically: yes   no

Notes:

PROPERTY #3

Street address:

City, state, zip code:

Owned by:

Type of residence: primary residence   vacation home

Purchase price: $

Purchase date:

Current value of property: $

Type of value: market   assessed

Source(s):

Property record attached or saved electronically: yes   no

Notes:

CO-OP

Street address:

City, state, zip code:

Property record attached or saved electronically for unit in NYC: yes   no

Sales price of other units currently for sale: $

Estimated value of prospect's unit: $

Source(s):

Notes:

Finding Salaries and Net Worth

5

I T WOULD BE great for prospect researchers if everyone's salary and net worth were publicly available. The problem is that this is almost never the case. Nevertheless, when you are researching a prospect, look for salaries for your prospect and the spouse/partner if they work outside of the home. In most instances you will be able to find only a range for the salary, but even a range is useful information and should be included in the prospect's research profile. To find where your prospect or his or her spouse/partner works, refer to the chapter on biographical information.

If your prospects are very wealthy, they may be included on a list of wealthy individuals or a list of millionaires or billionaires published by *Forbes* or another source. These lists include estimated net worth figures. It will be a rare occurrence to have one of your prospects appear on this list, but when one does appear on a wealthy list, it is key information to share with your library director or fundraising staff.

General Salary and Compensation Resources

There are several general resources that provide average salary amounts for most industries and professions in the United States. Once you have determined the employment information for your prospect and the spouse/partner, spend a little time researching the field to determine salary ranges for each industry discovered. Some professions have wider ranges than others; for instance, if your prospect is an insider in a publicly traded company, you will be able to find their salary. On the other hand, if your prospect is an artist, it will be very hard to determine his or her income. Additionally, the range of incomes for artists is large, so you will need to use other factors to make an educated guess. This chapter includes examples of some occupations, but is certainly nowhere near comprehensive.

The first place to start when researching a salary is often with the Bureau of Labor Statistics Wage Data (www.bls.gov/bls/blswage.htm), an excellent resource for the average salary amounts of given professions in different locations. This information is searchable by region, state, occupation, and industry. Industries are listed by the specific category name and the North American Industry Classification System (NAICS). You can find the NAICS number by searching for the company on Hoover's or another business reference source. Try several searches on the Bureau of Labor Statistics Wage Data website to gauge its accuracy for your region: look for average salaries for librarians and other occupations and industries, then look at the average salaries for people in your region and state. When you cannot find an exact salary for a prospect—which will be most of the time—this is a good option to use as an estimate of his or her salary.

O*NET OnLine (www.onetonline.org) is also an excellent starting point for finding average salary ranges and position descriptions, as well as expansive information about specific positions and industries and the projected rate of growth for the field. Try searching for "librarian" or "archivist" on this site to get an idea of the kind of information that is provided.

There are several other general resources that provide average salary amounts, including the salary calculator through CareerBuilder (http://salary.careerbuilder.com), Indeed (www.indeed.com), Glassdoor (http://www.glassdoor.com/index.htm), and Salary.com (www.salary.com/category/salary). Salary.com provides average salaries for positions in Canada as well as the United States. Take a look at these websites and try searching for specific job titles in the city or town where you live to get a feel for what information is provided; how the average salaries are calculated varies from website to website.

When you are researching a prospect, also search in news sources for articles that list average salaries for the professions you discover.

Some occupations have such a broad salary range that this information may not be as useful. Writers are a good example of this: some writers do not get paid at all or are paid very little for academic articles and similar publications, while a few writers get paid vast amounts for bestselling novels. Search for news articles on salaries for specific professions that will better explain how to determine where someone might fall within a salary range, and review your prospect's career history to put this information into perspective.

Attorneys' Salaries

Lawyers' and law firm partners' salaries can be found through the subscription-based American Lawyer (www.americanlawyer.com), which publishes annual lists of the top 100 and 200 law firms in the United States, with average compensation figures for attorneys and partners at these firms. If your library does not have access to that subscription, then you can find average salary ranges through the general websites listed in this chapter.

Physicians' Salaries

Physicians and surgeons salaries are compiled by the American Medical Group Association and available at Cejka Search (www.cejkasearch.com/physician -compensation-report). You have to register to view the information, but access is free. The Merritt Hawkins website (www.merritthawkins.com) also provides salary ranges for physicians and surgeons. To find salary ranges for people in the medical field and related fields, such as psychologists, search the "Job Salaries by Career Field" page provided on the Health Career Center (www .healthcareercenter.org/health-salaries.html).

Employees at Nonprofit Organizations

If you find out that a prospect you are researching is an employee of a nonprofit organization, or his or her spouse/partner is an employee, then you can take a look at the nonprofit's most recent 990 tax return. Nonprofit organizations file 990 tax returns, which may include salaries for the employees of the nonprofit. On the 990 tax return, "the organization must list up to 20 current employees who satisfy the definition of key employee (persons with certain responsibilities and reportable compensation greater than $150,000 from the organization and related organizations), and its five current highest compensated employees with reportable compensation of at least $100,000 from the organization and related organizations."[1] Compensation includes the salary and benefits for the employees.

Many 990 tax returns can be found for free online through the Foundation Center (http://foundationcenter.org/findfunders/foundfinder) or through GuideStar (www.guidestar.org) by searching under the organization's name and location. Scan through the 990 tax return to find the section that lists employees and their compensation to see if your prospect or his or her spouse/partner is listed. (More information on what is included on 990 tax returns and further information on nonprofit organizations is included in chapter 7.)

Faculty, Teacher, and Principal Salaries

If your prospect or his or her spouse/partner is a teacher, principal, or college professor, then you will be able to find salary ranges for him or her. Sometimes you can even find the exact salary amount. First, do a general Internet search for terms such as *teachers' salaries* and *Chicago*, which will produce results for salary ranges for teachers and administrators. You may need to include the school district in the search.

There are times when you can find exact faculty salaries by a simple Internet search; for example, search *"faculty salaries"* and the name of your alma mater and see what results you get. Next, try searching for faculty salaries on a university's or college's website. You can also find salary ranges on the *Chronicle of Higher Education*'s website, which provides faculty salaries compiled by the American Association of University Professors (http://chronicle.com/article/faculty -salaries-table-2012/131433); this information is searchable by state or by college or university name. You can also use the *Collegiate Times* website to find salaries for faculty at public universities (www.collegiatetimes.com/databases/salaries). Public universities, by their nature, make their salary information public, so you should be able to find the exact salary for an individual.

Public Officials and Civil Servants Salaries

Also due to the public nature of the information, you can find ranges or specific salaries for public officials and civil servants working at the city, state, or federal level. This will include, to name just a few examples, legislators, judges, the mayor of your city, and perhaps even the director of your library, depending on how your library is structured. How this information is accessed will vary from location to location, so for your city and state, check the city's and state's official websites to determine where this information can be found.

For federal employees, refer to the salaries and wages information provided on the Office of Personnel Management's website and select the "salaries and wages" option (www.opm.gov/policy-data-oversight/pay-leave). For some positions, you will need to know the grade or level for the position. Take a look at the website to see how to search it.

Another option for finding federal salaries is to search the government's job site, USA Jobs (https://www.usajobs.gov). Salary ranges are listed in the postings for open positions; search for a position that is similar to your prospect's position or a grade level that is the same. Use the advanced search to add the grade level, location, specific title, or government agency or department. Try searching for specific positions to see what is included in the job postings. To find out what government agencies have offices in your area, search for all positions in your state.

Executives' Salaries at Public and Private Companies

When your prospect or prospect's partner/spouse is an employee of a company, do some preliminary research before trying to find a salary—if the company is a public company, then you may be able to find the exact salary depending on the position in the company. The top five executives' salaries, their total compensation packages, and their stock holdings are public information. (Refer to chapter 6 to get detailed instructions on how to find this information.)

If the prospect or the prospect's spouse/partner works at a public company, but is not one of the top five executives at that company, then you will not be able to find any salary or stock information. The same is true for private company employees in any position, including the owner or chief executive officer, unless the information is published in a news source.

Once you determine that your prospect is an employee of a company, determine whether that company is public or private by searching Hoover's or another business reference source. You could also search for the company on Yahoo! Finance (http://finance.yahoo.com), or any other source that provides stock prices and ticker symbols for public companies. Basically, if the company is listed, then it is a public company; if it isn't, it is a private company.

Net Worth Estimates

A prospect researcher cannot make an estimate of a person's net worth. In order to determine net worth, one needs to know the value of all of someone's assets and debts. You will never get enough information to make this estimate. Nevertheless, some companies provide estimates on the net worths of the very wealthy. Companies estimate net worth though various means, and if they report the net worth of a prospect, you should use it. However, you should not estimate a prospect's net worth yourself.

The most famous estimates of net worth are provided by *Forbes*. *Forbes* publishes lists of the very wealthiest people that include rankings and estimates of their net worth. *Forbes*'s information is available for free online at *Forbes* (www.forbes.com). If your library has a subscription to this journal, you can monitor all the wealthy lists published by *Forbes* for any of the prospects or potential donors to your library. If any are on a *Forbes* wealthy list, then they should be your prime candidates for major gifts to your library, once you library director or fundraisers have established a relationship with them.

Subscription-based Wealth-X (www.wealthx.com) provides very detailed profiles and an estimate of net worth for people in the United States and abroad with an estimated net worth of $30 million or more. The profiles include employment and employment history, education, corporate and civic board memberships, and information on family members. What is really useful in the profile is the net worth figure calculated based on the person's assets. Also note, there are many people included in this database who are not on a *Forbes* wealthy list.

The Helen Brown Group website (www.helenbrowngroup.com/services/wealth-lists) provides wealthy lists and other lists of high-profile people in the United States and abroad. Review these lists to find prospects, trustees, volunteers, and donors to your library. And remember, general Internet and news searches can be a good way to find out whether a prospect is on a wealthy list.

Research Profile

In the research profile, include the salary or the salary range for your prospect and his or her spouse/partner, as well as the amount or range and the salary year. You should also mention the source, especially for exact salary figures. For a salary range, include further information that would be helpful in determining where your prospect might fall within that range if the salary is listed in a very broad range. You may not be able to determine exactly where your prospect will fall within the range, but you can state whether your prospect is likely to be at the lower or higher end based on the information you found on your prospect's career. (For example, is he or she writing articles for academic journals or writing bestselling novels?) Sometimes you will not be able to determine where your prospect falls within a salary range.

When your prospect or his or her spouse/partner is listed on a wealthy list, include this information in the research profile as well, with the source of the list, the year it was published, the net worth estimate for the prospect, and where he or she falls on the list (if the list is ranked by net worth).

PRACTICE EXAMPLE 1

Your library director would like you to find the salary for one of your prospects. She is a lawyer and works in a major law firm in your city.

- Your library has a subscription to *American Lawyer* (www.americanlawyer .com), so you start with this source. You check for the name of the law firm where your prospect works on the top 100 and the 200 law firms lists.
- Your prospect's firm is not listed, so you use one of the general salary sources to find ranges for lawyers in your area.
- You also search for your prospect and her firm in news sources, just in case there was an article published on her salary or salaries for lawyers who work at her firm.

PRACTICE EXAMPLE 2

You are researching a prospect's spouse who is a full professor at Ohio State University in the history department and want to include his salary in the research profile.

- You start by searching for the search terms *"faculty salaries"* and *"Ohio State University"* using an Internet search. This returns results through more than one source. You use *Collegiate Times* (www.collegiatetimes.com/databases/ salaries) and are able to search for the faculty member by name and get his exact salary.

ONLINE SOURCES

Fee-Based

American Lawyer .... **www.americanlawyer.com**
Provides annual lists of the top 100 and 200 law firms in the United States, with average compensation figures for attorneys and partners at these firms.

Hoover's .... **www.hoovers.com**
A business reference source used to find information about companies, the company address, annual sales, employees, and the North American Industry Classification System (NAICS). You can also use this source to determine whether a company is public or private.

Wealth-X .... **www.wealthx.com/home**
Provides very detailed profiles and net worth estimates for people in the United States and abroad with an estimated net worth of $30 million or more.

Free

Bureau of Labor Statistics .... **www.bls.gov/bls/blswage.htm**
Provides information on salaries and compensation; searchable by region, state, occupation, and industry.

CareerBuilder .... **http://salary.careerbuilder.com**
Provides a salary calculator searchable by position and location.

Cejka Search .... **www.cejkasearch.com/physician–compensation–report**
Provides average salaries for physicians and surgeons. The figures are compiled by the American Medical Group Association.

Chronicle of Higher Education .... **http://chronicle.com/article/**
faculty-salaries-table-2012/131433
Provides access to the faculty salary survey compiled by the American Association of University Professors. The survey is searchable by state, or by college or university name.

Collegiate Times .... **www.collegiatetimes.com/databases/salaries**
Provides salaries for faculty at public universities.

Foundation Center .... http://foundationcenter.org/
findfunders/foundfinder
Provides access to 990 tax returns for nonprofit grant-making organizations, which will list employees' compensation for those with salaries of a certain minimum amount.

Forbes .... www.forbes.com
Compiles wealthy lists with estimates of the net worth of people included on the lists.

Glassdoor .... www.glassdoor.com
Provides average salary amounts for positions. The results can be limited by location.

GuideStar .... www.guidestar.org
Provides access to 990 tax returns for nonprofit organizations, which will list employees' compensation for those with salaries of a certain minimum amount.

Health Career Center .... www.healthcareercenter.org/
health-salaries.html
Provides salary ranges for people working in the medical field and related fields, such as psychologists, art therapists, and dietitians, to name just a few examples.

Helen Brown Group .... www.helenbrowngroup.com/services/wealth-lists
Provides wealthy lists and other lists of high-profile people in the United States and abroad.

Indeed .... www.indeed.com
Provides average salary amounts for a broad variety of positions. The results can be limited by location.

Merritt Hawkins .... www.merritthawkins.com
Provides salary ranges for physicians and surgeons.

O*NET OnLine .... www.onetonline.org
Provides a large amount of information about specific positions and industries. A search for a job title will include information on salary ranges, position descriptions, educational requirements, traits needed for the position, and projected job growth in that field.

Office of Personnel Management .... www.opm.gov/policy
-data-oversight/pay-leave
Use the "Salaries & Wages" link to find salaries and wages for federal employees. Some positions are listed by the grade or level and other positions are listed by title.

Salary.com .... www.salary.com/category/salary
Provides average salaries for positions in Canada, as well as the United States.

USA Jobs .... https://www.usajobs.gov
Search this site for open government positions to find a position similar to your prospect's position or a grade level that is the same. Salary ranges are listed in the postings for open positions. The advanced search feature allows you to search by grade level, location, specific title, or government agency or department.

Yahoo! Finance .... http://finance.yahoo.com
Can be used to determine if a company is public or private. If searching under a company's name returns results that include a share price and a ticker symbol, then the company is public; if not, then the company is private.

NOTE

1. "Form 990 Part VII and Schedule J—Reporting Executive Compensation Frequently Asked Questions and Tips," Internal Revenue Service, May 26, 2012, www.irs.gov/pub/irs-tege/execcomptips_03252012.doc-stc_changes.pdf.

SALARIES AND NET WORTH WORKSHEET TEMPLATE

CONFIDENTIAL

PROSPECT'S NAME:

Researcher's name: Date:

PROSPECT

EMPLOYER #1:

Employer's address (city, state):

Prospect's business title:

Type of organization: for profit   nonprofit

Salary: $ range   estimate   exact figure

Source(s):

Notes:

EMPLOYER #2:

Employer's address (city, state):

Prospect's business title:

Type of organization: for profit   nonprofit

Salary: $ range   estimate   exact figure

Source(s):

Notes:

PREVIOUS EMPLOYER:

Employer's address (city, state):

Prospect's business title:

Type of organization: for profit   nonprofit

Salary: $ range   estimate   exact figure

Source(s):

Notes:

NET WORTH

Amount: $

Source and Date:

Rank on List:

PROSPECT'S SPOUSE/PARTNER

EMPLOYER #1:

Employer's address (city, state):

Spouse's/partner's business title:

Type of organization: for profit   nonprofit

Salary: $ range   estimate   exact figure

Source(s):

Notes:

EMPLOYER #2:

Employer's address (city, state):

Spouse's/partner's business title:

Type of organization: for profit   nonprofit

Salary: $ range   estimate   exact figure

Source(s):

Notes:

PREVIOUS EMPLOYER:

Employer's address (city, state):

Spouse's/partner's business title:

Type of organization: for profit   nonprofit

Salary: $ range   estimate   exact figure

Source(s):

Notes:

NET WORTH

Amount: $

Source and Date:

Rank on List:

Stock Holdings and Compensation for Prospects at Public Companies

ONE OF YOUR prospects might be a corporate insider at a United States public company. If so, this is great news for you, because you will be able to find a tremendous amount of financial information about that prospect. Information about corporate insiders' stock holdings in the company and their compensation must, by law, be submitted to the Securities and Exchange Commission (SEC). This valuable information about a person's compensation and insider stock holdings is public information, available to anybody. So, the first step in getting loads of financial information about your prospects is finding out if they work for or are board members of a public company.

Public Companies

A company is defined as public when it sells its securities, including stock, to the public through a stock exchange. A quick way to determine if a company is public is to search the company name using any free website that provides the current share price for companies sold on an exchange. Some examples are Yahoo! Finance (http://finance.yahoo.com), MarketWatch (www.marketwatch.com), or Bloomberg (www .bloomberg.com), but there are many more. If results are found when you search for the company name and there is a current share price listed for the company along with a ticker symbol, then you have confirmed that it is a public company. Try this search to get a feel for what the results look like: search for McDonald's (ticker MCD) or Hyatt Hotels Corporation (ticker H). Next, try searching for SC Johnson. (This company is private and has no listing.) You also can check to see if a company is public by referring to any business reference source, such as the subscription-based Hoovers (www .hoovers.com).

Corporate Insiders

Not everyone who works for a public company must submit filings with the SEC; only corporate insiders must provide information that is made public. "Corporate insiders—meaning a company's officers and directors, and any beneficial owners of more than ten percent of a class of the company's equity securities registered under Section 12 of the Securities Exchange Act of 1934—must file with the SEC a statement of ownership regarding those securities."[1] So, once you have confirmed that your prospect works for a public company, the next step is to find out if he or she is an insider of the company. If so, then his or her compensation and stock holdings with the company are public information.

Checking to see if your prospect is an insider takes a few simple steps. One way to do this is to search for the company name in Yahoo! Finance (http://finance.yahoo.com), then look at the "Insider Roster," found under "Ownership," to display a list of all of the corporate insiders for the company. Try this search using the Hershey Company (ticker HSY) or another public company as an example.

Another way to find out who the insiders are is by referring to a public company's website. Public companies often provide a list of the company's executive and corporate board members online, found under a heading such as "Investor Relations." This is usually located at the very bottom of the web page or at the top of the page in small print, under a heading of something similar to "About the Company." The board and executives will usually be listed under a heading such as "Corporate Governance" or "Leadership." This section should include a list of the corporate board members and the top executives, who may have SEC filings. Not everyone listed will be a corporate insider; check with the SEC filings to verify this information. How to do this is described in a later section of this chapter.

The company website may also include links to annual reports. Annual reports include financial information for the company and are useful to glance through. The company website may include some of the recent SEC filings as well. Look at public company websites, such as the investor relations sites for Target or Coca-Cola, for examples of public companies that include SEC filings on their websites.

Not all companies provide access to SEC filings on their websites, but there are other ways to access this information described in a later section of this chapter.

Proxy Statements

Once you have determined that your prospect is an insider (or to confirm that information), refer to the most recent proxy statement (SEC form DEF 14A) filed by the company. "It's called a 'DEF 14A' because it's the 'definitive,' or final, proxy statement. '14A' refers to the fact that proxy statements are filed pursuant to Section 14(a) of the Securities Exchange Act of 1934."[2] These comprehensive reports are filed annually by the company and include a lot of financial information about the company, as well as financial information about the corporate insiders affiliated with the company. A proxy statement includes biographical information along with information about total compensation, such as salary, perks, and stock holdings. (Perks are benefits that are treated as compensation but are not paid in cash, such as use of a corporate jet or use of a corporate car.) The proxy statement may also include compensation agreements for retirement or change of control agreements, for when the prospect leaves the company voluntarily or involuntarily.

Proxy statements are very long documents. Nevertheless, there are only a few sections that you will need to refer to in most cases. These sections are the biographical information about the prospect, the summary compensation table, the board member compensation, and the stock holdings sections—the sections you will regularly use to evaluate the wealth of your prospect.

If your prospect's name is listed in the section for compensation (or board member compensation) and the section on stock holdings in the proxy statement, then he or she is an insider. If your prospect is not listed in the compensation or stock holdings sections of the proxy statement, then he or she is not an insider; you will not be able to find any information about the prospect's compensation or stock holdings, because that is not public information.

Perhaps your prospect recently joined the company or was recently promoted. If this is the case, look at the most recent proxy statement to find out if the person who formerly held your prospect's position is an insider. If so, although you may not be able to find financial information for your prospect right away, eventually you will be able to. You may have to wait until the next proxy statement is filed. However, there is a SEC form called a form 8-K, which is similar to a press release for the company. Major events and news about the company are disseminated through 8-K forms; information about compensation is found in section 5.2 of the 8-K form. You can find 8-K forms through the same sources (described below) used to find proxy statements.

How to Find Proxy Statements

Proxy statements are available through the Securities and Exchange Commission's free database, EDGAR (electronic data gathering, analysis, and retrieval system; www.sec.gov/edgar.shtml). You can search for proxy statements under the company's name or the ticker symbol, found under "Search for Company Filings." Try this search using the name or stock symbol for a public company.

The results can be filtered by the form type. Enter *"DEF"* to limit the results to proxy statements. Look for the most recent proxy statement (DEF 14A) and select the hyperlink to view the document. Make sure you are not looking at a form called DEFA 14A. This is a different type of form that will be discussed later.

The EDGAR website allows searching by company name. It also allows keyword searching for individuals by entering a name into the company search field. However, this method must be used with caution. It works well for uncommon personal names, but a lot of results will be returned when searching for common names. For more common names, fee-based Morningstar Document Research (http://corporate.morningstar.com/us/asp/subject.aspx?xmlfile=6575.xml) provides searchable access to all SEC filings and allows you to search for individuals while limiting the results by company name. It is also possible to set up alerts for new proxy statements or other SEC filings that you may need to track.

Proxy statements found through EDGAR or Morningstar are searchable, just like a word document. So, you may wish to start by reviewing some proxy statements with the names of the CEOs and board members as examples. Browse through the document using the search function on your keyboard to find all the references to the CEO and a board member and look at the biographical information, compensation, stock holdings, and employment agreement. This is exactly how you will search proxy statements when you are doing prospect research.

Other Types of Proxy Statements

There are other types of proxy statements, such as the DEFA 14A or DEFR 14A, which include additional information (the A in DEFA is for "additional"), revised information (the R in DEFR), or some change to the most recent proxy statement. As a matter of course, you should glance at any other types of proxy statements filed after the most recent DEF 14A to make sure that the additional or revised information doesn't have to do with the compensation or stock holdings for your prospect.

Biographical Information in a Proxy Statement

Proxy statements usually include brief biographical information about the executives and the corporate board members. This is a good place to start when researching your prospect because it often lists other corporate and nonprofit boards he or she serves on. It also often includes information about the insider's education, career, age, and the length of affiliation with the company. Sometimes family relationships are also described, particularly if other family members are affiliated with or are insiders of the company. Board members usually serve for a term; the length of the term and when they will be up for reelection is included in this section of the proxy statement.

Compensation in a Proxy Statement

The compensation for the chief executive officer, the chief financial officer, and the next three highest-earning executives are listed on the proxy statement, as is the compensation for board members. "In the annual proxy statement, a company must disclose information concerning the amount and type of compensation paid to its chief executive officer, chief financial officer and the three other most highly compensated executive officers. A company also must disclose the criteria used in reaching executive compensation decisions and the degree of the relationship between the company's executive compensation practices and corporate performance. This information can be found in several separate disclosure items."[3]

Because proxy statements are filed annually, the compensation listed is for the previous year. Be sure to review the information about the compensation table and the footnotes. The compensation table includes the most recent base salary and possibly the past two years or three years as well. It also includes the bonuses, options awarded, retirement funds, and all other compensation, all of which is part of the total compensation package for executives. When it is time to fill out your research profile, list the most recent base salary and the total compensation as separate figures. Board members also receive compensation, and this information will be in the proxy statement as well. Read through some proxy statements to get a feel for how compensation information is displayed for executives and board members.

Employment Agreement and Change of Control in a Proxy Statement

In the filing, review the employment agreement section, also called the termination information or change of control information, to find out how the executive will be compensated if he or she leaves the company voluntary or involuntary. You may wish to read through this information as you research, but you might decide to include it in the research profile only when your prospect has left the company.

Stock Holdings in the Proxy Statement

Stock holdings for executive and board members are usually listed in the same table in the proxy statement and are found under "Beneficially Owned Stock," "Common Stock," or another similar heading. You will recognize it because the table will list the stock holdings for the corporate insiders. There might be several different kinds of stock holdings listed for each insider and a lot of footnotes further describing the stock holdings. If you are having difficulty understanding the terms used, the dictionary feature of the website, QFinance (www.qfinance

.com), is an excellent source for finding definitions of financial and stock-related terms. Refer to it if you run across a type of stock or a term that is not covered in this chapter.

You will want to separate the stock holdings into three categories: stock that is directly owned by the prospect (common stock); stock that is indirectly owned by the prospect (indirectly held common stock); and stock that has been granted, but will not be owned or available to be purchased until a future date, such as stock options, restricted stock, and phantom stock. The reason you want to track these separately is to add together similar types of stock holdings in order to come up with an approximately value for the stock.

The stock table will have a lot of footnotes and explanatory information, but once you have reviewed a few proxy statements, you will be familiar with how to interpret the information. The stock holdings information usually reflects stock holdings for your prospect near the date of the filing of the proxy statement. That date is listed in the proxy statement, either above or below it, in the footnotes of the stock table.

Common Stock

Common stock is one of the types of stock holdings listed in the stock table on the proxy statement. Common stock is the stock that your prospect owns directly and can sell at any time if he or she wishes to do so. Stock is defined by the website Motley Fool as "ownership of a corporation represented by shares that are a claim on the corporation's earnings and assets."[4]

Once you have the total number of directly held shares of stock owned by your prospect, calculate a value for the stock. To get a current vale for the stock, multiply the total number of shares by the current share price for the stock, which can be found through Yahoo! Finance (http://finance.yahoo.com), Bloomberg (www.bloomberg.com), MarketWatch (www.marketwatch.com), or some other source that provides current share prices for public stock. The number of shares and the current value of the stock should be included in the research profile.

Class A and Class B Stock

Some companies issue more than one type of common stock (Class A or Class B), usually based on voting rights for the stock. Class A typically grants voting rights, and Class B usually does not. To find out the specifications of the different types of common stock, refer to the company's bylaws or charter statement, on the company website under the investor relations section. As the share value is usually the same for Class A and Class B, for the purposes of prospect research, it is usually not necessary to know the specifications for the rights of the stock; it is only necessary if it affects the value of the stock.

Indirectly Held Stock

Common stock that is indirectly held will be identified as such in the footnotes in the stock holdings table. The stock is indirectly held because ownership is through someone else, such as a spouse or a family member, or through another entity, such as a trust or a retirement account. Because you will not be able to find any information about how a trust works or to confirm that your prospect is the sole beneficiary of the trust, it is best to consider this stock separately. Stock held in a retirement account will become accessible to the prospect upon retirement. You may wish to also provide values for stock held in trust and in a retirement account in the research profile. Board members will not, of course, have stock held in a retirement account, but may have indirectly held stock, held by a family member or held in trust. Directly held and indirectly held stock should be totaled separately in the research profile.

Stock Options

Stock options held by executives or board members will also be listed on the proxy statement. Stock options are shares that are available to be purchased in the future, once the options have vested (become available to be purchased). The purchase price and purchase date are set when the stock options are awarded. The Motley Fool points out, "An employee stock option is an option to purchase company stock offered to an employee usually either as compensation or as a performance incentive."[5] Stock options are the same for corporate board members.

The insider does not have to exercise (purchase) vested options but is likely to do so if the stock option price to purchase the options is lower than the market value for the shares on the day that the shares become available. Because the option price was set when the stock options were awarded, if the value of the stock increases, the insider will be able to purchase stock at a discounted amount. In other words, as the Motley Fool states, "a share of stock [is] purchased at a price lower than the current market price. From the moment of exercising the option, the newly received shares act just like any other shares of the company and can be kept or sold. The difference in those prices is taxable income to the employee and many times, the employee sells enough shares to cover the tax bill. The employee can either keep the rest or sell them on the market, pocketing the difference between the selling price and the exercise price."[6]

A proxy statement isn't the best or easiest way to find the price to purchase stock options or when they will be available to be purchased. This information is easier to find on a different form, SEC Form 4, described in a later section of this chapter.

List stock options for your prospect as a separate total in the research profile. Calculating the value of stock options is slightly more complicated because you have to subtract the purchase price from the current value of the shares. You may wish to also include the exercise dates—which is when the prospect is able to acquire the options—in the research profile, so that the gift officer or library director can plan to ask the prospect for a gift when he or she has just sold options.

Restricted Stock

Sometimes a company will give employees stock shares as a bonus. Unlike options, which must be paid for, these shares are given as a free reward. These shares are called restricted stock. The Motley Fool says, "Restricted stock constitutes shares granted to a company employee as a bonus. Unlike stock options, which employees must exercise in order to own and sell, restricted stock usually comes as a free award."[7] The restriction has to do with when the employee will receive the stock. "Restricted stock arrives in two phases, granting and vesting. When a company grants restricted stock, it promises you the delivery of shares at a predetermined date. The stock vests when the date arrives and the shares pass into your possession."[8] These shares should also be added separately and the vesting dates should also be included in the research profile.

Phantom Stock

There is another category that is similar to restricted stock called phantom stock. The Motley Fool states, "Restricted stock units are similar to phantom stocks. Another employee compensation program, phantom stocks constitute the promise to pay a bonus at a future date of equal value to a set number of company shares. Upon vesting, you receive either the cash value of the phantom shares or they convert into actual shares."[9] Because phantom stock will be granted as shares or cash at some point in the future, these shares should be counted with restricted shares. In the research profile, list the restricted stock and the phantom stock and mention the date when the shares will vest and convert into directly held common stock or cash.

SEC Form 4

In addition to proxy statements (DEF14A) that are issued annually, there is a different form that lists all other stock transactions that occurred for each insider between proxy statement filings. This is called SEC Form 4. It is important to look at these forms and to learn how to read them. These forms are issued within two business days of an insider making a stock transaction. The insider's name and title are listed at the top of the form.

There are two tables listed on the Form 4 (see figure 6.1). Table I, "Non-Derivative Securities Acquired, Disposed of, or Beneficially Owned," shows transactions for directly and indirectly held stock, indicated with D (for "directly held") or I (for "indirectly held") under "Ownership Form" in the table. The Motley Fool website points out, "This is where most of the important information is found. If the person is buying or selling shares or exercising options and

FIGURE 6.1 SEC FORM 4

You may not send a completed printout of this form to the SEC to satisfy a filing obligation. You can only satisfy an SEC filing obligation by submitting the information required by this form to the SEC in electronic format online at https://www.onlineforms.edgarfiling.sec.gov.

FORM 4

☐ Check this box if no longer subject to Section 16. Form 4 or Form 5 obligations may continue. *See* Instruction 1(b).

UNITED STATES SECURITIES AND EXCHANGE COMMISSION
Washington, D.C. 20549

STATEMENT OF CHANGES IN BENEFICIAL OWNERSHIP

OMB APPROVAL	
OMB Number:	3235-0287
Expires:	December 31, 2014
Estimated average burden hours per response:	0.5

(Print or Type Responses)

1. Name and Address of Reporting Person*			2. Issuer Name and Ticker or Trading Symbol		5. Relationship of Reporting Person(s) to Issuer (Check all applicable)
(Last)	(First)	(Middle)	3. Date of Earliest Transaction Required to be Reported (Month/Day/Year)	4. If Amendment, Date Original Filed(Month/Day/Year)	___ Director ___ 10% Owner ___ Officer (give title below) ___ Other (specify below)
(Street)					6. Individual or Joint/Group Filing (Check Applicable Line) ___ Form filed by One Reporting Person ___ Form filed by More than One Reporting Person
(City)	(State)	(Zip)			

Table I — Non-Derivative Securities Acquired, Disposed of, or Beneficially Owned

1. Title of Security (Instr. 3)	2. Transaction Date (Month/Day/Year)	2A. Deemed Execution Date, if any (Month/Day/Year)	3. Transaction Code (Instr. 8)		4. Securities Acquired (A) or Disposed of (D) (Instr. 3, 4 and 5)			5. Amount of Securities Beneficially Owned Following Reported Transaction (s) (Instr. 3 and 4)	6. Ownership Form: Direct (D) or Indirect (I) (Instr. 4)	7. Nature of Indirect Beneficial Ownership (Instr. 4)
			Code	V	Amount	(A) or (D)	Price			

Reminder: Report on a separate line for each class of securities beneficially owned directly or indirectly.
* If the form is filed by more than one reporting person, *see* Instruction 4(b)(v).

Potential persons who are to respond to the collection of information contained in this form are not required to respond unless the form displays a currently valid OMB control number.

(Over)
SEC 1474 (11-11)

FORM 4 (continued)

Table II — Derivative Securities Acquired, Disposed of, or Beneficially Owned
(*e.g.,* puts, calls, warrants, options, convertible securities)

1. Title of Derivative Security (Instr. 3)	2. Conversion or Exercise Price of Derivative Security	3. Transaction Date (Month/Day/Year)	3A. Deemed Execution Date, if any (Month/Day/Year)	4. Transaction Code (Instr. 8)		5. Number of Derivative Securities Acquired (A) or Disposed of (D) (Instr. 3, 4, and 5)		6. Date Exercisable and Expiration Date (Month/Day/Year)		7. Title and Amount of Underlying Securities (Instr. 3 and 4)		8. Price of Derivative Security (Instr. 5)	9. Number of derivative Securities Beneficially Owned following Reported Transaction (s)(Instr. 4)	10. Ownership Form of Derivative Security: Direct (D) or Indirect (I) (Instr. 4)	11. Nature of Indirect Beneficial Ownership (Instr. 4)
				Code	V	(A)	(D)	Date Exercisable	Expiration Date	Title	Amount or Number of Shares				

Explanation of Responses:

** Intentional misstatements or omissions of facts constitute Federal Criminal Violations.
   See 18 U.S.C. 1001 and 15 U.S.C. 78ff(a).

**Signature of Reporting Person   Date

Note: File three copies of this Form, one of which must be manually signed. If space is insufficient, *see* Instruction 6 for procedure.

Potential persons who are to respond to the collection of information contained in this form are not required to respond unless the form displays a currently valid OMB Number.

Page 2

selling those, this is where it is found. Plus, the person must list how many shares are owned after each transaction."[10] So, the purchase or sale of directly held stock will be listed in this table or when stock options are purchased and sold. This table will also show if or when an insider moves directly held stock into a trust. Each transaction is reported on a separate line of the form.

Table II, "Derivative Securities Acquired, Disposed of, or Beneficially Owned (e.g., puts, calls, warrants, options, convertible securities)," shows transactions for other types of stock, such as options, phantom stock, and restricted stock. This table also lists the conversion or exercise price of the shares and dates when the options can be exercised or the phantom or restricted stock will be vested.

When stock options vest (are available to be purchased), those options will be listed in Table II. If the insider purchases those options, they convert to common stock, and that transaction is listed in Table I, as a common stock purchase. Often the next transaction listed in Table I is the sale of those options (now common stock), sold at the higher current share price.

A Form 4 usually will have a lot of footnotes with additional information about the stock and you will want to read through them closely to get additional information about the stock holdings. Understanding a Form 4 takes a little practice, so review a few of them, looking at both tables to get a feel for how the information is displayed. Refer to the general instructions for filing out a Form 4 to get more information about the form and to find the transaction code list for the transaction types listed on the Form 4. This document can be found on the EDGAR website (www.sec.gov/about/forms/form4data.pdf). The Edgar website has a description of all of the other SEC filing types as well, and can be found here: www.sec.gov/about/forms/secforms.htm.

Form 3

A Form 3 is filed when a person becomes an insider. According to the SEC, "The initial filing is on Form 3. An insider of an issuer that is registering equity securities for the first time under Section 12 of the Exchange Act must file this Form no later than the effective date of the registration statement. If the issuer is already registered under Section 12, the insider must file a Form 3 within ten days of becoming an officer, director, or beneficial owner."[11]

Form 5

A Form 5 is filed when information was not previously included on a Form 4 and should have been. The SEC states, "Insiders must file a Form 5 to report any transactions that should have been reported earlier on a Form 4 or were eligible for deferred reporting. If a Form must be filed, it is due 45 days after the end of the company's fiscal year."[12]

How to Find Forms 3, 4 and 5

These forms are found through EDGAR (www.sec.gov/edgar.shtml) by searching on the company's name and selecting to include Forms 3, 4, and 5 in the search (ownership). You can also find these forms through the subscription-based Morningstar Document Research (http://corporate.morningstar.com/us/asp/subject.aspx?xmlfile=6575.xml).

How to Calculate the Value of Stock Holdings

Calculate the value of the directly held stock by multiplying the number of shares by the current stock price, which can be found through Yahoo! Finance (http://finance.yahoo.com), Bloomberg (www.bloomberg.com), MarketWatch (www.marketwatch.com), or your preferred source. It is the same process for indirectly held stock.

It is also the same process to calculate the value of direct stock as it is of phantom stock and restricted stock, but those figures are estimates on the value, because the share price might be higher or lower when the prospect actually receives the stock or the cash. Stock options also have an estimated value and require the additional step of subtracting the purchase price from the share price.

Other Sources for Finding Insiders' Stock and Compensation

Subscription-based EquilarAtlas (www.equilar.com/atlas) compiles stock holdings and compensation for individuals in a report. These reports may also include biographical information and nonprofit affiliations for the prospect. It is possible to set up alerts on your prospects (who are in the EquilarAtlas database) so that new information about those prospects' stock acquisitions are forwarded directly to you via e-mail.

IPOs and SEC Form S-1

Stock holdings and compensation for prospects working at or on the boards of private companies is not public information. However, this information becomes public when a private company becomes public through an initial public offering (IPO).

An IPO is the first time that a company offers stock for sale to the public. There will be several articles in the press about each stage of this process. When a company is going to go public, a Form S-1, the registration statement, is filed with the SEC. This document provides a detailed financial statement about the company, including compensation for the top executives of the company.

The number of shares to be offered and the share price, based on the value of the company, are determined just before the date of the IPO. Once the company is public, then the share price fluctuates, as it does with all public companies. You may wish to look at the news articles and Form S-1 filings for the IPOs for Groupon, Facebook, Hyatt, or Google to get an idea of how to find this information. If you are researching a prospect affiliated with a private company that has filed a Form S-1, review that form to find the compensation information for him or her.

The Research Profile

When one of your prospects is a corporate insider at a public company, review the proxy statement (SEC Form DEF 14A) and include in the research profile any biographical information that you did not find through another source. You should also include in the research profile, their compensation information; base salary and total compensation, listed as two separate figures; and information about how the prospect will be compensated if he or she leaves the company, if this is relevant. You may wish to wait to include this information until the prospect has left the company.

Review the information about the prospect's stock holdings listed in the DEF 14A and check to see if there have been more recent Form 4s filed for your prospect, to find the most up-to-date information about their stock holdings. Calculate the value of their stock holdings, by finding the current value of their shares using a website that provides stock values. The capacity rating will be based on the directly held shares of stock, but all stock holdings should be included in the research profile. List separate totals for directly held common stock, indirectly held stock, stock options, restricted stock and phantom stock. You also may wish to include in the research profile the dates when options, restricted stock and phantom stock will vest.

PRACTICE EXAMPLE 1

The CEO of Cargill is a potential prospect for your library. Your library director would like to know the compensation and stock holdings for the CEO.

- For your first step, you find the name of the CEO of Cargill by looking at the company's website.
- Next, you check to see if Cargill is a public company by looking at the company's website or by searching for the company name in Yahoo! Finance (http://finance.yahoo.com) or another source, which provides stock information. You also consider using a business reference source, such as Hoovers, to find out if the company is public.
- You determine that Cargill is a private company. You will not be able to find compensation or stock information unless it has been reported through a news source. That information is not filed with the SEC and is not publicly available.

PRACTICE EXAMPLE 2

The fundraising staff at your library scheduled a meeting with a director (corporate board member) of Hershey and would like to know the prospect's stock holdings in Hershey and when the prospect joined the board.

- You check to see if Hershey is a public company by looking at the company website. Hershey is a public company.
- You find the most recent proxy statement for Hershey using either EDGAR (www.sec.gov/edgar.shtml) or Morningstar Document Research (http://corporate.morningstar.com/us/asp/subject.aspx?xmlfile=6575 .xml). You find the biographical information listed for your prospect, including the date when she joined the board.
- You search in the proxy statement for the table showing stock holdings and note the stock holdings listed in the proxy statement.
- You find a more recent SEC Form 4 that has been filed for the prospect. You use the stock holdings listed on the Form 4, as those figures are more current than the proxy statement.

PRACTICE EXAMPLE 3

You are researching an executive vice president at Google and would like to find the prospect's compensation and stock holdings.

- Your first step is to confirm that Google is a public company, through the company website, a reference source or a web source that lists public stock. Google is a public company.
- Next, you find the most recent proxy statement to find the compensation information for your prospect.
- Your prospect was recently hired, so you find out whether the position your prospect has is an insider's position by finding the name of the person who previously held the position. It is an insider position. You are able to find the compensation information for your prospect on a SEC Form 8-K or on a future proxy statement filing.

PRACTICE EXAMPLE 4

Your library director would like to know the compensation for the CEO of a private company that has just announced an upcoming IPO.

- You verify that the company is going to go public by checking news sources and by searching EDGAR for the SEC Form S-1 filing for the company.
- The company filed an S-1 form, where you find the compensation for the CEO in that document.

ONLINE SOURCES

Fee-based

EquilarAtlas .... www.equilar.com/atlas
Compiles stock holdings and compensation for individuals in a report. Alerts
can be set up on your prospects and you will receive e-mail messages about any
changes in their stock holdings, based on SEC filings.

Hoovers .... www.hoovers.com
A business reference source used to check if companies are public or private.

Morningstar Document Research .... http://corporate.morningstar.com/
us/asp/subject.aspx?xmlfile=6575.xml
Provides access to all SEC forms and is searchable by personal name. You can set
up alerts on prospects as well.

Free

Bloomberg .... www.bloomberg.com
Used to confirm that a company is public and to find the current share price for
public company stock.

Edgar .... www.sec.gov/edgar.shtml
Provides access to SEC forms; searchable by company name and keyword.

MarketWatch .... www.marketwatch.com
Used to confirm that a company is public and to find the current share price for
public company stock.

QFinance .... www.qfinance.com
Provides a dictionary for financial and stock terms.

SEC Forms .... www.sec.gov/about/forms/secforms.htm
Complete list, with descriptions, of all SEC forms.

SEC Form 4 Guidelines www.sec.gov/about/forms/form4data.pdf
This PDF gives a more thorough explanation of what is included on a Form 4.

Yahoo! Finance .... http://finance.yahoo.com
Used to confirm that a company is public, to find the current share price for public company stock, and to get a list of the corporate insiders at a company. A list of insiders can be found, once you have searched for a company, by selecting the link to "Insider Roster" under "Ownership," which will display a list of all the corporate insiders for the company.

NOTES

1. "Forms 3, 4, 5," US Securities and Exchange Commission (SEC), last modified January 15, 2013, www.sec.gov/answers/form345.htm.
2. "How Do I Obtain a Copy of a Company's Annual Proxy Statement?" US Securities and Exchange Commission, last modified August 14, 2003, www.sec.gov/answers/proxyhtf.htm.
3. "Executive Compensation," US Securities and Exchange Commission, last modified September 2, 2011, www.sec.gov/answers/execomp.htm.
4. "Stock," *Dictionary of Finance Terms* [Barron's Educational Series, 2006], accessed April 23, 2013, www.credoreference.com.turing.library.northwestern.edu/entry/barronsfin/stock.
5. "Employee Stock Option," Motley Fool, accessed April 29, 2013, http://wiki.fool.com/Employee_stock_option.
6. "The Life Cycle of an Option," Motley Fool, accessed April 29, 2013, http://wiki.fool.com/Employee_stock_option.
7. "Restricted Stock," Motley Fool, accessed April 27, 2013 http://wiki.fool.com/The_Difference_Between_a_Restricted_Stock_Unit_%26_Restricted_Stock_Award.
8. "Granting and Vesting," Motley Fool, accessed April 27, 2013 http://wiki.fool.com/The_Difference_Between_a_Restricted_Stock_Unit_%26_Restricted_Stock_Award.
9. "Restricted Stock, Phantom Stocks and Stock Options," Motley Fool, accessed April 28, 2013 http://wiki.fool.com/The_Difference_Between_a_Restricted_Stock_Unit_%26_Restricted_Stock_Award.
10. "Form 4," Motley Fool, accessed May 26, 2013, http://wiki.fool.com/Form_4.
11. "Forms 3, 4, 5" US SEC.
12. "Forms 3, 4, 5" US SEC.

STOCK HOLDINGS AND COMPENSATION RESEARCH WORKSHEET TEMPLATE

CONFIDENTIAL

PROSPECT'S NAME:

Researcher's name: Date:

STOCK HOLDINGS

PUBLIC COMPANY NAME:

Ticker symbol:

Prospect's or spouse's/partner's position with company:

DEF 14A (proxy statement):   yes   no

Form S-1 (IPO filing):   yes   no

Prospect or spouse/partner is listed on DEF 14A or S-1:   yes   no

Date on SEC filing:

Form 4:   yes   no

Date on form:

Notes:

Other SEC Forms that were consulted (e.g., 8-K or Form 3 or 5):

Current share price of stock: $

Source:

COMMON STOCK

Total number of shares of directly held common stock:

Current value: $

Sources: DEF 14A   Form 4

Total number of shares of indirectly held common stock:

Current value: $

Held by (e.g., trust, spouse, other family members):

Sources: DEF 14A   Form 4

STOCK OPTIONS

Number of stock options:

Purchase price: $

Current value (current share price minus purchase price): $

Vesting date:

Number of stock options (different purchase price from above):

Purchase price: $

Current value: $

Vesting date:

RESTRICTED STOCK

Number of restricted stock:

Current value (current share price): $

Vesting date:

Number of restricted stock (different vesting date from above):

Current value: $

Vesting date:

PHANTOM STOCK

Number of phantom stock:

Vesting date:

Current value: $

COMPENSATION

Base salary: $

Salary year (usually year prior to filing):

Total compensation package: $

Change of control or employment agreement:

Source(s):

Notes:

SEC FORMS

Attached to worksheet or saved electronically (list forms and dates):

_____

_____

_____

Family Foundations

S OMETIMES FAMILIES HAVE charitable foundations that make donations to worthy causes. This means that your library could get funding from these family foundations, because family members determine who gets the family foundation's money. So, it is important to know if a prospect has a family foundation. It is also helpful to know for other reasons, such as determining the types of organizations and causes the family foundation typically supports. This chapter describes how to find and identify a prospect's family foundation.

A foundation is a nonprofit organization that makes donations to other nonprofit organizations. A family foundation has family members on the foundation board, and the board members determine which nonprofits will receive donations. A family foundation's assets can be used to help determine how to evaluate the prospect's capacity and potential giving to your library. The sole purpose of a foundation is to make donations to nonprofit organizations, so knowing that an individual has a family foundation will help your library director get those foundation gifts directed to your library.

Foundations

The definition of a foundation is "a nonprofit organization that supports charitable activities to serve the public good. Foundations are often created with endowments-money given by individuals, families, or corporations. They generally make grants or operate programs with the income earned from investing the endowments."[1] A foundation is required by law to give a portion of assets, earned from investing the endowment, each year to other nonprofit organizations; "a private foundation must meet or exceed an annual payout requirement of five percent of the average market value of its net investment assets in order to avoid paying excise taxes."[2] This means that foundations must make a minimum amount of cash donations per year, based on assets, or will have to pay additional taxes to the government as a penalty.

There are several types of foundations, and all of them are described in this chapter. The terms used to describe different types of foundations can be a little confusing. Ultimately, it is the Internal Revenue Services and the US tax code that define and determine what is and what is not a foundation. Some of the types of foundations are also defined separately by the IRS, and some are distinctions made only by fundraisers; family foundations fall into this latter category.

Private Foundations versus Family Foundations

The IRS does not make a distinction between a family foundation and a private foundation. The terms *private foundation*, *independent foundation*, and *family foundation* all mean the same thing to the IRS. These terms are used interchangeably by the fundraising community as well. The tax code is the same for all foundations, but they are not the same when considering an individual's potential giving to your library. The essential distinction for fundraising purposes is that a family foundation has family members, including the prospect you are researching, who serve on the board and determine which nonprofit organizations will receive donations. Because the board members are related to each other, there is more flexibility for them to determine where to direct the foundation giving. It is also possible for your fundraising staff or your library director to form relationships with, or cultivate, all the family board members to facilitate a gift to your library from a family foundation.

On the other hand, a private nonfamily foundation has unrelated board members and also may have a hired staff, and may require a grant application to apply for a grant. A family foundation may also have paid staff members and grant guidelines, of course, so the most important distinction is that they have family members on the board. Sometimes there is a mix of unrelated and related board members, so you will have to make a judgment call on whether you think it is a family foundation. You will also have to decide if the grant guidelines seem inflexible, in which case, the foundation should not be treated as a family foundation.

An example of a family foundation is the Allyn Foundation (www .allynfoundation.org), which has mostly family members serving on the board. The foundation is described as a family foundation on the website as well. An example of a private foundation is the John D. and Catherine T. MacArthur Foundation (www.macfound.org), which has both unrelated board members and paid staff members. There are no MacArthur family members on the board or staff. The foundation is described on the website as an independent foundation. This can be particularly confusing because most private foundations start out as family foundations. Review the websites of these two foundations to get a feel for the difference between a family foundation and a private or independent foundation. Soon you will easily be able to recognize a family foundation.

Of course, any source of funding should be included in the fundraising strategy for your library. However, in the case of individual prospects, only a family foundation that your prospect is directly affiliated with should be used to calculate his or her potential giving. The reason is that a prospect with a family foundation has greater control over where the gifts are directed; gifts are likely to be given without requiring a grant application. The assets of a family foundation were given by the family. A gift from a foundation is more likely to be given when the library director or fundraising staff have a relationship with a donor or a potential donor. By comparison, a private foundation cannot be used as a wealth indicator unless the prospect you are researching is a paid employee of the foundation. The reason is that a private foundation will adhere to its grant guidelines. Although a close relationship with a trustee might help somewhat in considering a grant application from your library, if the grant does not adhere exactly to foundation grant guidelines, your grant will not get funded.

None of this is an exact science, of course, so it will be necessary to work with your library director or fundraisers to determine how to proceed.

How to Find Family Foundations

Now that you know how to identify a family foundation, the next step is determining if the person you are researching has one. Subscription-based access to the Foundation Center (www.foundationcenter.org) and to GuideStar (www .guidestar.org) will allow you to search under trustees' names to find out if your prospect has a family foundation when you do not know the name of the organization. If your prospect is on the board of the foundation or is a donor to the foundation, you will be able to find the name of the family foundation using these databases, and the foundation type will be identified for you.

When you do not know the name of a prospect's family foundation, or to check to see if your prospect might have one, you can search for the foundation by assuming that the prospect's name is part of the foundation name and limit the search results to the city where he or she lives. This can be done by using any of the free-access sources GuideStar or the IRS (www.irs.gov/Charities-&-Non-Profits/ Exempt-Organizations-Select-Check), or the limited free version of the Foundation Center (http://foundationcenter.org/findfunders/foundfinder). The Foundation Center also provides searching by key word, an option for finding trustees listed in the 990s. If you find results through your search, you still should verify that you have found the prospect's family foundation by looking at the IRS form 990 tax return. How to do this is also described in a later section of this chapter.

How To Find Family Foundations for Donors

If your prospect has already given to your library in the past, you can review the giving history to see if there have been gifts made through organizations for which the donor has received credit in some way, such as being sent a thank-you letter for the gift. If your library has a system in place to track donors and donations, then this should be fairly easy to do. Also review a donor's giving history to see if your donor's name is generally associated with a gift from a foundation. If your library does not have a system in place, then the library director or the fundraising staff may know that the donor makes gifts to the library through an organization.

If you find out that your donor makes gifts through an organization and you have the name of that organization, there are a few more steps to determine what type of organization it is. It is not possible to determine the type of entity or organization it is simply by its name. An organization with the name "John Smith Family Foundation" is not necessarily a family foundation, a foundation at all, or even a tax-exempt organization. It could be any number of things, such as a charity, a trust, a donor-advised fund, or a corporate foundation. (All of these types of organizations are described later in this chapter.)

How To Identify a Nonprofit

When you know the name of an organization, you can determine the type of organization it is by taking a few simple steps. Firstly, determine if the entity is a nonprofit organization by searching for it under the organization's name using the free nonprofit lookup feature in GuideStar or through free access to the Foundation Center.

You can also search for a nonprofit entity for free by using the Internal Revenue Service (IRS) website, under the "Exempt Organizations Select Check" feature (www.irs.gov/Charities-&-Non-Profits/Exempt-Organizations-Select-Check). Enter the city and state of the organization. If you get too many results, try entering the organization's name in quotes to narrow down your results. The name of the organization will display on the screen with the location. Each website works slightly differently, so try them each out with the name of a foundation that you know.

It is also possible to search for some nonprofits in Canada, Israel and Mexico through the IRS. The United States has tax treaties with these countries that allow for donations to the listed organizations to be tax deductible, based on qualifications of both the donor and the foreign nonprofit organization. Refer to IRS Publication 526 for more information on this subject.

IRS Nonprofit Codes

Under the exempt organizations search on the IRS website described above, the results list will include the name of the organization, the location, and a code. Once you have returned results following a search, you can click on the code to get a description of it, which indicates what type of nonprofit it is. A private foundation has the code PF (private foundation), and that is how all family foundations are coded as well. Public charities (defined in a later section) have the code PC. Private operating foundations are code POF. Try this search using the Allyn Foundation as an example.

Public Charities

If the organization is listed by the IRS, then it has some level of tax-exempt status. If it is a charitable organization, then it is categorized as either a charity or a foundation. GuideStar says, "Charitable organizations . . . fall under Section 501(c)(3) of the U.S. Tax Code. The Internal Revenue Service divides charitable organizations into two groups: private foundations and public charities."[3] Unlike a foundation that receives its funding from just a few sources, usually family members, a public charity receives its funding from multiple sources. According to Grantspace, "Public charities generally derive their funding or support primarily from the general public, receiving grants from individuals, government, and private foundations. Although some public charities engage in grantmaking activities, most conduct direct service or other tax-exempt activities."[4] *If the entity is a public charity, then it should not be considered a wealth indicator for your prospect.* This is because your prospect and your prospect's family will not be the only funding sources for the charity, and therefore will not be able to make direct decisions about what the charity funds.

Aside from those already listed, there are other types of exempt organizations, which fall under section 501(c) of the tax code, including social welfare organizations (501(c)(4)), agricultural/horticultural and labor organizations (501(c) (5)) and business leagues or trade associations (501(c)(6)).[5] If your prospect is affiliated with one of these types of tax-exempt entities, that information can be collected to reflect his or her interests, but these entities are not family foundations.

Operating Foundations

There are two other types of nonfamily foundations to be aware of: operating foundations and corporate foundations. The IRS does identify operating foundations, but not corporate foundations. The IRS indicates if a foundation is an operating foundation. An operating foundation is "[an] endowed private foundation that uses the bulk of its income to provide charitable services or to run charitable programs of their own (such as a school or camp). Operating foundations make few, if any, grants to outside organizations. To qualify as an operating foundation, specific rules, in addition to the applicable rules for private foundations, must be followed."[6] The assets from an operating foundation should not be used to calculate a prospect's potential giving and should be viewed only as an indication of philanthropic interest. It is also unlikely that your library would receive a grant from an operating foundation, unless it is the operating foundation that supports your library.

Corporate Foundations

A corporate foundation, like a family foundation, is not identified as such by the IRS; both types are considered private foundations. However, it is fairly simple to determine that a foundation is a corporate foundation, because a corporate foundation gets its funding from a company and has company employees on the foundation board. Corporate foundations usually have grant application guidelines. Look at the Coca-Cola Foundation using a Foundation Center search as an example of a corporate foundation. Corporate foundations should not be considered when determining a prospect's wealth, even when the company is a private company and the prospect is the owner of the company. The reason is that the prospect will not have the same level of influence over foundation giving as with a family foundation. There will be exceptions to this, of course, so work with your library director to determine how to proceed if it is unclear.

IRS Form 990 Tax Return

Once you have determined that an organization is a foundation, and you have determined that it is a family foundation, review the foundation assets and the foundation giving. This is done by consulting the foundation's IRS form 990 tax return. All foundations must file a 990 tax return. Many of these filings can be found for free online through the Foundation Center or GuideStar by searching under the foundation name and location. You cannot get 990 returns from the IRS website.

Some nonexempt trusts are treated as a private foundation; this is determined by the entity filing a 990 tax return. If you find a 990 for a nonexempt trust, then you can treat the trust exactly as you would a foundation. These are different from trusts that do not file 990 tax returns referred to in a later section.

On a 990 tax return form, the fair market value of assets is listed on the first page of the tax return and is found a few lines under the name of the organization (see figure 7.1). The amount of grants paid out within the filing year is listed on line 25, also on the first page. Any assets given to the foundation totaling $5,000 or more made by one person or entity must also be listed on the 990 tax return that is found under parts I and II. These gifts are usually made by the foundation trustees. All gifts and grants made by the foundation, including amounts and names of the recipients, are also listed on the return, and that information is usually found toward the end of the tax return form. The highest paid foundation employees' names and salaries at a certain level are also listed on a 990 tax return. This is useful if you are researching a staff member of a private foundation. (Refer to chapter 5 for more information on finding salaries and net worth.)

FIGURE 7.1 FORM 990-PF

Form **990-PF**

Department of the Treasury
Internal Revenue Service

Return of Private Foundation
or Section 4947(a)(1) Nonexempt Charitable Trust
Treated as a Private Foundation
Note. The foundation may be able to use a copy of this return to satisfy state reporting requirements.

OMB No. 1545-0052

2011

For calendar year 2011 or tax year beginning   , 2011, and ending   , 20

Name of foundation	A Employer identification number
John Doe Family Foundation	

Number and street (or P.O. box number if mail is not delivered to street address)	Room/suite	B Telephone number (see instructions)
200 State Street		

City or town, state, and ZIP code

Anytown, USA 12345

C If exemption application is pending, check here ▶ ☐

G Check all that apply: ☐ Initial return ☐ Initial return of a former public charity ☐ Final return ☐ Amended return ☐ Address change ☐ Name change

D 1. Foreign organizations, check here . . . ▶ ☐
2. Foreign organizations meeting the 85% test, check here and attach computation · · ▶ ☐

H Check type of organization: ☑ Section 501(c)(3) exempt private foundation
☐ Section 4947(a)(1) nonexempt charitable trust ☐ Other taxable private foundation

E If private foundation status was terminated under section 507(b)(1)(A), check here . . . ▶ ☐

I Fair market value of all assets at end of year (from Part II, col. (c), line 16) ▶ $ **$500,000**

J Accounting method: ☐ Cash ☐ Accrual
☐ Other (specify) _____
(Part I, column (d) must be on cash basis.)

F If the foundation is in a 60-month termination under section 507(b)(1)(B), check here · ▶ ☐

Part I Analysis of Revenue and Expenses (The total of amounts in columns (b), (c), and (d) may not necessarily equal the amounts in column (a) (see instructions).)

		(a) Revenue and expenses per books	(b) Net investment income	(c) Adjusted net income	(d) Disbursements for charitable purposes (cash basis only)
Revenue	1 Contributions, gifts, grants, etc., received (attach schedule)				
	2 Check ▶ ☐ if the foundation is **not** required to attach Sch. B				
	3 Interest on savings and temporary cash investments				
	4 Dividends and interest from securities				
	5a Gross rents				
	b Net rental income or (loss)				
	6a Net gain or (loss) from sale of assets not on line 10				
	b Gross sales price for all assets on line 6a				
	7 Capital gain net income (from Part IV, line 2) . .				
	8 Net short-term capital gain				
	9 Income modifications				
	10a Gross sales less returns and allowances				
	b Less: Cost of goods sold . . .				
	c Gross profit or (loss) (attach schedule)				
	11 Other income (attach schedule)				
	12 **Total.** Add lines 1 through 11				
Operating and Administrative Expenses	13 Compensation of officers, directors, trustees, etc.				
	14 Other employee salaries and wages				
	15 Pension plans, employee benefits				
	16a Legal fees (attach schedule)				
	b Accounting fees (attach schedule)				
	c Other professional fees (attach schedule) . . .				
	17 Interest				
	18 Taxes (attach schedule) (see instructions) . . .				
	19 Depreciation (attach schedule) and depletion . .				
	20 Occupancy				
	21 Travel, conferences, and meetings				
	22 Printing and publications				
	23 Other expenses (attach schedule)				
	24 **Total operating and administrative expenses.** Add lines 13 through 23				
	25 Contributions, gifts, grants paid	$25,000			
	26 **Total expenses and disbursements.** Add lines 24 and 25				
	27 Subtract line 26 from line 12:				
	a **Excess of revenue over expenses and disbursements**				
	b **Net investment income** (if negative, enter -0-) .				
	c **Adjusted net income** (if negative, enter -0-) . . .				

For Paperwork Reduction Act Notice, see instructions.   Cat. No. 11289X   Form **990-PF** (2011)

Foundation Giving Requirements

The US tax code requires that foundations give approximately 5 percent of the average market value of its assets each year. This means that your library could get up to 5 percent of a family foundation's assets each year. Calculating the 5 percent payout is complicated, so using the most recently reported market value (line i on form 990) and taking 5 percent of that amount is a sufficient method to enable you to calculate the maximum amount a family foundation could give to your library. This means that if you find the most recent foundation assets, which are listed on the 990 tax return, you can project what a foundation could potentially give to your library as roughly 5 percent of the most recent foundation assets for one year (or you can project for a multiyear gift). A foundation can give more than the required 5 percent of assets, so you can also make this calculation based on the average foundation giving over the past five years by reviewing the previous 990 tax returns for the foundation. Look up several 990 tax returns using either Guidestar or the Foundation Center to get familiar with where the information is listed on the return and how to read the return. The Foundation Center also provides a tutorial on reading 990 tax returns.

Other Types of Entities

Any organization listed on the IRS website has some level of tax-exempt status. The results for an organization will display an IRS code indicating what type of organization it is. If an organization is not listed by the IRS then either it may not be a tax-exempt organization, or it could be a donor-advised fund or a trust. Depending on what the organization is, you may not be able to find any more information about it. It may also be difficult to determine what kind of organization you have when it is not listed by the IRS.

Donor-Advised Funds

A donor-advised fund, as defined by the Internal Revenue Service, is "a separately identified fund or account that is maintained and operated by a section 501(c)(3) organization, which is called a *sponsoring organization*. Each account is composed of contributions made by individual donors. Once the donor makes the contribution, the organization has legal control over it. However, the donor, or the donor's representative, retains advisory privileges with respect to the distribution of funds and the investment of assets in the account."[7]

When your library receives a gift from a donor-advised fund, the gift usually includes a letter from the operating organization, such as a community foundation. If your library receives a check from a community foundation (or another type of nonprofit organization) and there is an accompanying letter naming the donors who directed a gift to your library, then you know that the gift was made through a donor-advised fund. This is actually the only way you will find out that your donor has a donor-advised fund, unless the donor tells your library director or the fundraising staff. There is no further information you can find on the donor-advised fund, except that it exists and which nonprofit administers it. You will not be able to find any more information on your donor's donor-advised fund—not the assets of the fund, when it was established, or any other recipients of gifts from the fund.

Trust Funds

There also is not any public information on trust funds. A trust fund is "property (e.g., money or securities) held in a trust; that is, property held legally by one party (the legal owner) for the benefit of another party (the equitable owner). The legal owner, or trustee, has the right of possession and the right of use of the property, but must exercise those rights to the benefit of the equitable owner, or beneficiary."[8] You will not be able to determine any information about the trust—not the terms of the trust, the amount in the trust, or who is affiliated with the trust.

Nonprofit Board Memberships

Sometimes prospects are on boards of public charities or foundations other than their family's foundation. Participation on a nonprofit board by your prospect is important information to collect because it reflects his or her philanthropic interests and may help your library director facilitate a gift based on the individual's interests. In fact, participation on all nonprofit boards is worth including in the writeup about a prospect, as it will show the philanthropic interests of the individual. (Refer to chapter 9 for more information on memberships and affiliations.)

The Research Profile

When your prospect has a family foundation, include in their research profile the name of the foundation; the address of the foundation; and the board members and their relationship to the individual you are researching, if those relationships can be determined. Working from the most recent 990 tax return, list the foundation assets, the total giving from the foundation for that year, and the recipients of gifts and the amounts. If that is a very long list, you may wish to list the largest ten gifts. You should also include donations made by the prospect or his or her spouse to the family foundation.

PRACTICE EXAMPLE 1

Your library director would like to know if John Doe has a family foundation.

- You have a subscription to the Foundation Center, so you search for John Doe as a trustee and any foundations he is affiliated with.
- You look at each foundation listed to determine if it is a family foundation.

PRACTICE EXAMPLE 2

Your library director receives a gift from the Robert W. Wilson Charitable Trust and would like to know the assets of the organization and if it is a family foundation.

- You check the IRS website, the Foundation Center or GuideStar to find out what kind of organization it is. It is a foundation, even though the word *foundation* is not included in the name. So, it's not a charity and it's not a trust. That's good news. You can't yet tell if it is a family foundation, because the IRS doesn't make that distinction. You need to do a little more research to find out what kind of foundation it is.
- To find the assets, you look at the 990 tax return for the foundation. You find this through Guidestar or the Foundation Center, because you cannot get 990 returns from the IRS website. The most recent assets of the foundation are found on the first page of the most recent 990 tax return. Now you know the assets of the foundation, but you still don't know if it is a family foundation.
- As of 2010, the most recent 990 tax return lists Robert Wilson was the only trustee of the foundation, so the Robert W. Wilson Charitable Trust is a family foundation. You know that it's a family foundation because it is controlled by a family member.

PRACTICE EXAMPLE 3

Your library director finds out that a donor to your library is on the Heifer International Foundation board and would like to know more about that organization.

- You look at the website of the foundation to verify that your donor is on the board.
- You verify what kind of organization it is through the IRS website. It is a public charity. This means that it cannot be used to calculate a person's capacity to give, but you can use it to gauge the donor's interest.

PRACTICE EXAMPLE 4

The fundraising staff received a check and a letter stating that the William Jones Foundation has directed a gift to your library. The letter is from the Cleveland Community Foundation. The fundraisers would like to know the assets of the foundation.

- Because the letter is coming from a foundation that is different from the donor's foundation, this tells you that the William Jones Foundation actually is a donor-advised fund. The assets of the donor-advised fund are not public information. Therefore you cannot find any more information about it
- The Cleveland Community Foundation manages the donor-advised fund. The assets of the Cleveland Community Foundation are public, but irrelevant in terms of William Jones's assets or wealth.

PRACTICE EXAMPLE 5

Your library director would like to know how a donor is affiliated with the MacArthur Foundation and if the MacArthur Foundation is a family foundation.

- You review the foundation website to find how the donor is affiliated with the MacArthur Foundation. Staff and trustees are listed on the website. Looking at the website for a foundation is the best way to determine who is on the board and staff.
- Because no one on the board is related to each other and there are established grant guidelines, you determine that this is not a family foundation.
- You also check to see if your donor is one of the highest-paid employees of the foundation; his salary is listed on the most recent 990 tax return for the foundation.

PRACTICE EXAMPLE 6

The library receives a gift from Laura and John Arnold Foundation in Houston, Texas, and would like to know the assets of the foundation and if it is a family foundation.

- You search on the IRS's website for the Laura and John Arnold Foundation to verify that it is a foundation, which it is.
- You find the foundation's 990 tax return through Guidestar or the Foundation Center. Reviewing the 990 tax return shows the most current assets.

- The board of the foundation is a mix of related and paid staff. However, the most recent 990 tax return also shows that Laura and John Arnold made a donation to the foundation. This could go either way between a family foundation or a private foundation, so a discussion with your library director or fundraisers is necessary to determine if you should use this foundation as a wealth indicator for Mr. and Mrs. Arnold.

ONLINE SOURCES

Fee-based

Foundation Center .... www.foundationcenter.org
Allows searching by trustee name when you do not know the name of the family foundation. It is also a source to use to verify that your prospect has a family foundation.

GuideStar .... www.guidestar.org
Allows searching by trustee name when you do know the name of the family foundation.

Free

Foundation Center...http://foundationcenter.org/
findfunders/foundfinder
Provides access to 990 tax returns of nonprofit organizations and tutorials on how to read a 990 tax return.

GuideStar .... www.guidestar.org
Provides access to 990 tax returns of nonprofit organizations.

Internal Revenue Service .... www.irs.gov/
Charities-&-Non-Profits/Exempt-Organizations-Select-Check
Allows you to verify that an organization is a nonprofit and if so, what kind. Also provides plenty of useful information on nonprofit organizations.

NOTES

1. "Grantmaking FAQs: What Is a Foundation?" Forum of Regional Association of Grantmakers, accessed March 20, 2013, www.givingforum.org/s_forum/doc .asp?CID=25&DID=6158.

2. "What Is a 'Payout Requirement' for a Foundation?"Grantspace, accessed March 20, 2013, www.grantspace.org/Tools/Knowledge-Base/Funding-Resources/ Foundations/Payout.

3. "Just What are Public Charities and Private Foundations Anyway?" GuideStar, last revised August 2001, www.guidestar.org/rxa/news/articles/2001-older/just-what -are-public-charities-and-private-foundations-anyway.aspx.

4. "What Is the Difference between a Private Foundation and a Public Charity?" Grantspace, accessed March 20, 2013, http://grantspace.org/Tools/Knowledge -Base/Funding-Research/Definitions-and-Clarification/Private-foundations-vs -public-charities.

5. "Life Cycle of an Exempt Organization," IRS, last revised August 24, 2012, www.irs.gov/Charities-&-Non-Profits/Life-Cycle-of-an-Exempt-Organization.

6. "Glossary of Terms, Operating Foundation," Donors Forum, accessed March 20, 2013. www.donorsforum.org/s_donorsforum/sec.asp?CID=11767&DID=26561.

7. "Donor-Advised Funds," IRS, last revised September 6, 2012, www.irs.gov/ Charities-&-Non-Profits/Charitable-Organizations/Donor-Advised-Funds.

8. *Merriam-Webster Online,* s.v. "trust fund," accessed March 20, 2013, www.merriam -webster.com/dictionary/trust%20fund.

FAMILY FOUNDATION RESEARCH WORKSHEET TEMPLATE

CONFIDENTIAL

PROSPECT'S NAME:

Researcher's name: Date:

FAMILY FOUNDATION

Foundation Name:

Street address:

City, state, zip code:

BOARD MEMBERS

List name and relationship to prospect:

DATE OF 990 FILING:

FOUNDATION GIVING TOTAL: $

FOUNDATION ASSETS: $

5% OF FOUNDATION ASSETS: $

LIST RECIPIENT ORGANIZATION AND AMOUNT:

$

$

$

$

$

Prospect's or spouse's/partner's giving to foundation: $

Source(s):

990 Tax return attached or saved electronically?   yes   no

Notes:

CHARITIES

CHARITY NAME:

Street address:

City, state, zip code:

Purpose of charity (e.g., funds cancer research):

Prospect's position with charity (e.g., chair of board of trustees):

Source(s):

Notes:

TRUST, DONOR-ADVISED FUND, CANNOT DETERMINE ENTITY TYPE

ENTITY NAME:

City, state, zip code:

Determined entity type: yes   no

Notes:

Source of finding out about entity (e.g., made gift to library, listed in bio):

Source(s):

Notes:

Giving to Other Nonprofits and Political Donations

DEALLY, YOUR PROSPECTS have a history of giving to nonprofit institutions. You will want to research gifts made by your prospect or your prospect's spouse/partner to nonprofit institutions. (How to find gifts made through family foundations is covered in chapter 7.) Gifts given to other organizations indicate the interests of your prospect and the giving level at which the prospect gives. For instance, if you find that your prospect makes annual gifts of $1,000 to the local art museum, then the library director knows that a gift of $1,000 is not outside the prospect's comfort level and that he or she is interested in art. Your library director might ask the prospect for donations to purchase art books for the library. It's also important to find any political donations made by your prospect because this will also give your library director and fundraising staff an idea of the interests of the prospect.

Giving to Other Nonprofits

The first step to starting this research is to determine your prospect's spouse's or partner's name. It's important to research giving from spouses or partners as well as from your prospect. However, giving by other family members should not be included in the research profile on your prospect. as it doesn't necessarily reflect your prospect's interests or giving ability.

Subscription-based NOZA (https://www.nozasearch.com) compiles gifts given by individuals and is searchable by personal name. The search can be filtered to find results by a number of criteria. For instance, you can include the location of the institution that received the gift, but you cannot find gifts by the location of your prospect's home city or state. Because you cannot restrict your search to the location of the prospect, if your prospect has a common name, you may not be able to confirm whether the gift was given by him or her. Search NOZA with the prospect's name and the prospect's spouse's or partner's name. If both names appear for a gift, it is likely to have been made by your prospect. Sometimes there isn't enough information to verify that a gift was given by your prospect, so you will have to do more research to confirm it.

Internet Searching and News Sources

There are times when gifts to nonprofit institutions can be newsworthy, and the story will be picked up by a local paper or the institution will put out a press release. The best way to find information about gifts is by searching the Internet and a database of news sources, such as Proquest (www.proquest.com), Factiva (www.dowjones.com/factiva), or EBSCOhost (www.ebscohost.com) using the search terms of your prospect's name and then the spouse's or partner's name. If you get too many results, add the terms *gift, donation, pledge,* or *endowment* (and also try variations of these terms). These terms are not the same, and it's good to know the differences between them. *Gift* and *donation* mean the same thing. A pledge is a promise to make a gift, often paid over a period of time. Wayne State University points out, "An Endowed Fund is a fund established in accordance with donor wishes from which gift amounts (frequently referred to as 'Principal,' 'Corpus,' or 'Historic Dollar Value') cannot be spent. Endowed Funds are established 'in perpetuity' (in other words, indefinitely or until the donor wishes or agrees to terminate the fund)."[1]

Donors often like having their names attached to things. Institutions offer naming rights to prospects who are willing to make sizable gifts. Once something is named, information about it can usually be found on the Internet. When a donor endows a professorship, a chair, or a scholarship fund at a college or a university, it is often named in honor of the donor. So, if you find a named fund or faculty position named for your prospect or prospect's spouse/partner, dig a little further. Try searching on the university's or college's website for press releases about the establishment of the fund or faculty position. You should follow these steps for anything named for your prospect or his or her spouse/partner at a nonprofit institution, such as a gallery at a museum or a building on a college campus. You may not be able to find the amount of the gift, but you should still look for it. It never hurts to try.

Annual Reports

If you find gifts made by your prospect, or his or her spouse/partner, then you should review the annual reports for the institutions that received the gifts. Nonprofit institutions' annual reports often are available on the institution's website. Grantspace says, "The nonprofit annual report, although not a legal requirement, is often a valuable communications tool for nonprofits to get the message out about their activities over the course of the past year or years. It may also be the only published document that lists and recognizes donors to the organization, as this information is not required in the Form 990, the annual nonprofit information return required by the IRS."[2] If the institution does provide annual reports on its website, then find the section of the annual reports that lists gifts made by donors. You won't be able to find the exact amount of a gift, but the gifts will be reported in ranges, such as $1,000 to $5,000. The donors who made gifts at each gift range level will be listed. Search through the annual reports for your prospect's name and spouse's or partner's name.

Most gifts are not reported on in the news, so you may wish to do this search even if you haven't found a news article mentioning a gift made by your prospect for the institutions in your area. Glance through annual reports that are available on the websites of nonprofit institutions in your city. The name of the donor and the gift range will be listed, but the purpose of the gift or what it was directed to will not be included. To get a feel for what's included in a nonprofit annual report, look at the annual reports available online for the Cleveland Museum of Art (www.clevelandart.org/about/annual-report) or the Museum of Fine Arts in Boston (www.mfa.org/about/annual-report).

Most nonprofit institutions provide annual reports. The exception to this is a house of worship. It is often difficult to find gifts made to synagogues, churches, and mosques, as this information usually is not shared publicly. While many places of worship have newsletters, they rarely include information about donations made or giving levels.

Political Contributions

Prospects may give to political candidates or organizations. This is great for you because political donations of $200 or more are required by law to be made public. Political contributions of $200 or more can be found through the free resources OpenSecrets (www.opensecrets.org) or Follow the Money (www.followthemoney.org), or directly through the Federal Election Commission's transaction query by individual contributor page (www.fec.gov/finance/disclosure/norindsea.shtml). The FEC points out, "The FECA [Federal Election Campaign Act] requires candidate committees, party committees and PACs [political action committees] to file periodic reports disclosing the money they raise and spend. Candidates must identify, for example, all PACs and party committees that give them contributions, and they must identify individuals who give them more than $200 in an election cycle."[3] There are legal limits on how much an individual can contribute as well. For more information on this subject, refer to the "Citizen's Guide" on the FEC website (www.fec.gov/pages/brochures/citizens.shtml).

Each website differs in how the information is searched and presented. The advanced search option on OpenSecrets allows you to search by the name of the donor and limit your results to the state or zip code where the donor lives or works. Follow the Money includes local political gifts and also has an advanced search option that allows you to limit by state and by year. The FEC provides an advanced search that allows you to limit the search by state, zip code or employer. Try searching all these websites using the name of someone you know who made political donations of $200 or using a common last name.

Research Profile

In the research profile, include all the gifts that you can find for your prospect and your prospect's spouse/partner. List the gift amounts or gift ranges, the years the donations were made, and the institutions that received the gifts. If it is unclear what the purpose of the nonprofit is or the type of institution it is, you may wish to also include a brief explanation of what the institution does as well.

You should also list all the political contributions that you find for your prospect and your prospect's spouse/partner. Include the candidate who received the contribution or the PAC and the party affiliation, the amount of the contribution, and the year it was given.

PRACTICE EXAMPLE 1

Your library director notices that the rose garden in the local botanic garden is named in honor of one of your library donors and asks you to verify that it is named for the library donor and not a relative of his or someone with the same name. The library director also would like to know the amount of the gift and the year it was given to the botanic gardens.

- You begin by confirming the name of the rose garden through the botanic garden's website.
- Once you confirm the name of the garden and verify that it is the same name as your library donor, you search the Internet and news databases using the prospect's name and the botanic garden as search terms. An article published about the gift gives you enough detail to confirm that the garden was named in honor of your donor, along with the date of the gift.
- Next, you look through the annual report for that year on the botanic garden's website; you also search the website for a press release about the gift. The annual report includes a gift range (the purpose of the gift or what the gift was made in support of will not be included).
- Because a naming gift is a major gift and in this case was made as a pledge to be paid over a few years, you provide the total giving that you can find for the donor to the botanic garden, as part or all of that giving was made to name the rose garden.

PRACTICE EXAMPLE 2

The fundraising staff would like to know the largest single gift made to a non-profit by your prospect.

- As your library has a subscription to NOZA (https://www.nozasearch .com), you start there and search using your prospect's name and your prospect's partner's name, keeping track of all the results you find.
- Next you search through news sources and the Internet searches with the search terms of your prospect's name, her partner's name, and *gift, donation, endowment,* and *pledge* (and the variations of all these terms). You compare your results with what you found in NOZA.
- Finally, you look at the most recent annual reports for the nonprofit institutions in the area and review the prospect's giving to your library. It is possible that the single largest gift was given to your library, so you check the giving to your library as well. Of course it isn't possible to be certain that you have found all the gifts made by your prospect, so of the gifts that you were able to find, you determine which is the largest gift.

PRACTICE EXAMPLE 3

Your library director is hosting a luncheon for a few library donors who are very vocal about their political views, and wants to make sure that everyone will get along at the lunch. The library director would like to know if a library donor made a gift in the last presidential campaign and if so, to which candidate.

- You check the free resources that provide information on political contributions: OpenSecrets (www.opensecrets.org), Follow the Money (www.followthemoney.org), and the Federal Election Commission's transaction query by individual contributor page (www.fec.gov/finance/ disclosure/norindsea.shtml). You search for donations made by your donors and their spouses or partners, and record the information that you find.
- You next search the Internet and news sources using the search terms of your donors and their spouses' or partners' names. You find that one of the donors is the head of the finance committee for a candidate; that's important information. It's also good to know that another donor's spouse hosted a fundraising event for that same candidate.

ONLINE SOURCES

Fee-based

NOZA .... https://www.nozasearch.com
Provides information on gifts given by individuals to nonprofit institutions. The information is searchable by name, and the results can be limited by the location of the nonprofit institution.

Proquest .... www.proquest.com
Provides access to news sources to find information about gifts made by your prospect to nonprofit institutions that were reported on in the news.

EBSCOhost .... www.ebscohost.com
Provides access to news sources to find information about gifts made by your prospect to nonprofit institutions that were reported on in the news.

Factiva .... www.dowjones.com/factiva
Provides access to news sources to find information about gifts made by your prospect to nonprofit institutions that were reported on in the news.

Free

Federal Election Commission .... www.fec.gov/
finance/disclosure/norindsea.shtml
Provides information on political contributions of $200 or more and allows advanced search options to limit the results by state, zip code, or employer. This source also provides access to the FEC filing, which includes name of the employer of the donor.

OpenSecrets .... www.opensecrets.org
Provides information on political contributions of $200 or more and allows advanced searching by the state or zip code where the donor lives or works, and by year of the contribution.

Follow the Money .... www.followthemoney.org
Provides information on political contributions of $200 or more, with a focus on local political gifts. The advanced search option allows you to limit the results by state and by year.

NOTES

1. "Endowment Funds," Wayne State University, accessed June 15, 2013, http://idrm.wayne.edu/endowment/funds.php.
2. "Where Can I Learn More About Making a Nonprofit Annual Report?" Grantspace, accessed June 15, 2013, http://grantspace.org/Tools/Knowledge-Base/Nonprofit-Management/Accountability/Annual-reports.
3. "The FEC and the Federal Campaign Finance Law," Federal Election Commission, updated January 2013, www.fec.gov/pages/brochures/fecfeca.shtml.

NONPROFIT GIFTS AND POLITICAL CONTRIBUTIONS RESEARCH WORKSHEET TEMPLATE

CONFIDENTIAL

PROSPECT'S NAME:

Researcher's name: Date:

NONPROFIT GIFTS

RECIPIENT ORGANIZATION:

Amount of gift: $ Date of gift:

Source(s):

Notes:

RECIPIENT ORGANIZATION:

Amount of gift: $ Date of gift:

Source(s):

Notes:

RECIPIENT ORGANIZATION:

Amount of gift: $ Date of gift:

Source(s):

Notes:

RECIPIENT ORGANIZATION:

Amount of gift: $ Date of gift:

Source(s):

Notes:

POLITICAL CONTRIBUTIONS

CANDIDATE'S NAME OR PAC:

Party affiliation (e.g., Democrat, Republican, Independent, Green Party):

Amount of contribution: $ Date of contribution:

Source(s):

Notes:

CANDIDATE'S NAME OR PAC:

Party affiliation:

Amount of contribution: $ Date of contribution:

Source(s):

Notes:

CANDIDATE'S NAME OR PAC:

Party affiliation:

Amount of contribution: $ Date of contribution:

Source(s):

Notes:

PROSPECT'S SPOUSE/PARTNER NONPROFIT GIFTS

RECIPIENT ORGANIZATION:

Amount of gift: $ Date of gift:

Source(s):

Notes:

RECIPIENT ORGANIZATION:

Amount of gift: $ Date of gift:

Source(s):

Notes:

RECIPIENT ORGANIZATION:

Amount of gift: $ Date of gift:

Source(s):

Notes:

RECIPIENT ORGANIZATION:

Amount of gift: $ Date of gift:

Source(s):

Notes:

PROSPECT'S SPOUSE/PARTNER POLITICAL CONTRIBUTIONS

CANDIDATE'S NAME OR PAC:

Party affiliation (e.g., Democrat, Republican, Independent, Green Party):

Amount of contribution: $ Date of contribution:

Source(s):

Notes:

CANDIDATE'S NAME OR PAC:

Party affiliation:

Amount of contribution: $ Date of contribution:

Source(s):

Notes:

CANDIDATE'S NAME OR PAC:

Party affiliation:

Amount of contribution: $ Date of contribution:

Source(s):

Notes:

Memberships and Affiliations in Clubs and Other Organizations

YOUR PROSPECTS AND their spouses or partners may be members, trustees, and board or committee members of various organizations and clubs. It's important to identify these affiliations and memberships because they will give you a good idea of what your prospect and his or her family is interested in. This information will help the library director or fundraising staff identify the types of projects the prospect may want to fund at your library. Some of these affiliations and memberships can also be used as indicators of wealth. For instance, country and golf club memberships can be very expensive, so these memberships are another indicator that the prospect is wealthy.

A prospect's memberships and affiliations may also identify who your prospect is likely to know personally and who might know your prospect. If one of your library's trustees or volunteers belongs to the same golf club or nonprofit board as your prospect, then that library contact can assist with helping your library director or fundraising staff get to know the prospect and help with the cultivation of the prospect. This can help immensely in turning a prospect into a donor to your library.

Searching for Memberships and Affiliations

There are several ways to find memberships and affiliations. Memberships or affiliations might be listed in a prospect's bio on the prospect's employer's website or on the prospect's profile on LinkedIn (www.linkedin.com), if he or she has a profile there. This information might also be found through a news source, such as an article about the prospect or through a biographical resource, such as subscription-based Marquis Who's Who (www.marquiswhoswho.com). Reviewing all these sources should be part of your process when researching a prospect. You will also learn about memberships and affiliations if the prospect reveals this information to a gift officer or the library director. Try to verify the membership or affiliation by looking at the organization or club's website.

Another method of finding memberships and affiliations is to start with organizations in your city or community and review the organizations' websites for lists of members or board members. Look for names you recognize, such as your library's trustees, donors, and volunteers. Many types of organizations—such as museums, country clubs, or religious organizations—do not list their members through public sources. Nevertheless, they usually list board members, if the organization has a board. If you find out that a new library prospect is on the same board or affiliated with the same organization as a trustee, donor, or volunteer of your library, include that relationship in the research profile.

Nonprofit or For-Profit Clubs and Organizations

It is useful to know if an organization is for profit or is a nonprofit. This information will help you describe the organization when you mention the affiliation or membership in the prospect's research profile. This information will also guide your research. Determining that an organization is for profit will prompt you to look for membership costs to join the organization, as that information might be an indicator of wealth, if membership dues are expensive.

Finding memberships and affiliations to nonprofit organizations should direct you to search for gifts to the organization from your prospect and his or her spouse/partner. However, you may not be able to find membership fees to some types of nonprofit and tax-exempt organizations, as you would with the membership fees to an art museum or a zoo. More information on finding gifts to charitable organizations can be found in the giving to other nonprofits and political donations chapter.

To determine if an organization is for profit or nonprofit, search by the organization's name using the Internal Revenue Service (IRS) website, under the "Exempt Organizations Select Check" feature (www.irs.gov/Charities-&-Non-Profits/Exempt-Organizations-Select-Check). Click on the radio button to select organizations that "are eligible to receive tax-deductible contributions." Then search for the organization by entering the organization's name in quotation marks; include the city and state where the organization is located to narrow down the results. If the organization has chapters, then search by the name of the parent organization. For example, you would search for the Special Libraries Association (SLA) in Alexandria, Virginia, instead of Michigan's chapter of SLA.

Following your search, if you do not get any results, then the organization is most likely a for-profit organization. If you do return results, the list will include the name of the organization, the location, and a code. Click on the code, which will identify what type of organization it is. Public charities have the code PC; private foundations have the code PF. (Refer to chapter 7 for more information on this subject.)

The Internal Revenue Service has a specific exempt designation for fraternal orders: "lodge" or "group." They are in a separate category from charities and foundations. Fraternal orders are described later in this chapter.

Nonprofit Memberships and Board Memberships

Nonprofit organizations include charities, such as the American Red Cross, and museums, historical societies, zoos, botanic gardens and other libraries, to name just a few examples. These types of organizations are probably familiar to you because most libraries are nonprofit organizations. (For more information on charities, refer to chapter 7.)

When you are researching a prospect and see that a nonprofit membership or board affiliation is listed for him or her (or the spouse/partner) in a bio, it is a good idea to confirm this information to make sure it is still current. You should be able to find nonprofit board memberships—such as trustee appointments, advisory board appointments, and women's board memberships—on the nonprofit institutions' web pages. This information may be found under "About Us" or something similar on the nonprofit's website. The list of trustees should also be included in the most recent annual report for the institution, which is often provided online on the organization's website. You may also be able to find this information by searching the subscription-based versions of the Foundation Center (www.foundationcenter.org) or GuideStar (www.guidestar.org). Both of these sources will allow you to search by trustee name. The focus of the Foundation Center is grant-making organizations, so charities and other types of nonprofit organizations that do not make grants to other nonprofits may not be listed. The scope of GuideStar is a little broader, so both foundations and charities should be included there.

Not only do trustees and other types of board members volunteer their time to an institution, they very often also make gifts to the institution. In fact, many institutions tacitly require their board members to donate in order to remain on the board. So, once you have confirmed that a prospect or a prospect's spouse/partner serves on the board of a nonprofit, look for gifts made by the prospect or the prospect's spouse/partner to that institution. You can do this by reviewing the annual reports for that institution and searching for gifts made by the prospect or the prospect's spouse/partner. These will be found toward the end of the annual report. Gifts are listed in ranges, such as $5,000 to $9,999, with the donors who gave at that level listed alphabetically below each range. (Further information on how to research giving to other institutions is included in chapter 7.)

Lists of members of nonprofit institutions, such as museum memberships or memberships to the zoo, are not listed on the nonprofit's website or through annual reports, so the only way to find this information is if it is listed in publicly available biographical information on your prospect or your prospect's spouse/partner.

Civic, Service, Private, Social, and Special-Interest Clubs and Fraternal Orders

Civic, service, private, social, and special-interest clubs, as well as fraternal orders, are in a separate category from nonprofit organizations because some of these types of clubs and organizations are nonprofits and some are not. These clubs often have membership fees or dues and may also have a formalized application process to join, such as requiring nomination by current club members. A description of what is required to join is often included on the organization's website.

After reading several bios on your prospects, you will get a feel for recognizing and identifying civic, service, social, private, and special-interest clubs and fraternal orders. There is overlap between these categories of clubs and fraternal orders, of course, but having categories should help to make identifying them a little easier. Look at the websites of the clubs and organizations mentioned in the paragraphs below to see how to recognize and identify them. Look for these types of clubs and fraternal orders in your town or community as well. When you see a club or order membership or affiliation mentioned in a bio or a news article on your prospect, take a look at the organization's website to determine what type of club or order it is. Look for fees or dues for members, as sometimes membership fees and dues are very expensive and this information can be another wealth indicator for your prospect. The fees, dues, and membership requirements may not be public information, but it is always worthwhile to look.

Civic and Service Clubs

These clubs have a civic or service focused mission and support a specific cause or causes. Examples of civic and service clubs include Rotary International, Kiwanis International, Lions Clubs International, and the Junior League. Look at the websites for these organizations to get an idea of what a civic or service club does and how to identify them. Most civic and service clubs are charities and do not have barriers to joining, such as a nomination requirement by a current member or members. Often the local chapters of these clubs will not provide a list of members, but board members may be listed on the website. Usually you will have to rely on this information being provided directly by the prospect to your library director or the fundraiser, or finding it through a publicly available bio.

Private and Social Clubs

Private and social clubs usually have an elegant club building that includes a restaurant, a gym, and meeting rooms and serves as a hotel for members. Some of these clubs have private art collections, libraries, or other amenities for members. Some private clubs also have a civic or service component as well. Most social and private clubs require nomination from a current member and membership approval to join. What is required to join will usually be found on the club's website under "Membership."

Examples of private and social clubs are the Union League Clubs, located in Chicago, New York, and Philadelphia; the Metropolitan Club in New York (and other cities); the Algonquin Club of Boston; the Columbia Club of Indianapolis; and the Jonathan Club of Los Angeles. Most if not all of these types of clubs will not provide the names of members. If there is a board for the club, the board members may be listed on the club's website. You should look for this information and also search for membership fees and dues, as it is very likely to be a wealth indicator. Check for membership fees on the club's website and through news sources. You will also want to be become familiar with any private or social clubs in your community.

Special-Interest Clubs

There are many different types of clubs with a focus on the arts, politics, or some other special interest that is the focus of the club. Examples of special-interest clubs include the Caxton Club of Chicago and the Grolier Club of New York, both of which are clubs for book collectors and bibliophiles. The National Arts Club of New York focuses on fine arts. The World Affairs Council focuses on international affairs; there are chapters all over the country. Special-interest clubs often require nomination and approval for membership by current club members. Most of these clubs will not provide lists of members, but may provide board members or trustees' names on the club website. You should look for the costs to join and annual dues for these clubs, as they might serve as an indicator of wealth for your prospect.

Fraternal Orders

Although referred to here as fraternal orders, these organizations do not all exclude women from joining, but many do. These organizations may have religious affiliations. They may or may not be tax-exempt organizations. (Check the IRS website to determine if the fraternal order is tax exempt.) Fraternal orders have formalized procedures for joining and may be by invitation only from a current member of the order. Fraternal orders also have some unifying goal, theme or mission; what is required to join and the mission of the order will be listed on the website. Review this to get an idea of what the organization does and how to join it.

Examples of fraternal orders are the Knights of Columbus, Moose International, the Independent Order of Odd Fellows, Shriners International, and the Benevolent and Protective Order of Elks. Look at the websites for these organizations to get a better sense of how to identify fraternal orders. Most of these organizations do not publicly share their members' names, so in most cases you will learn about your prospect's affiliation with a fraternal order because it is listed in his or her bio. Nevertheless it is worth looking at the website of the local chapter, just in case more information is listed there.

Athletic Clubs and Country Clubs

This category doesn't refer to the local fitness club or gym. It includes exclusive clubs, such as yacht clubs, golf clubs, or country clubs, which usually have some application requirements for membership, such as being nominated by one or more existing members and significant membership fees and dues. Information on how to join should be listed on the website, but fees usually are not listed.

Examples of such clubs are Augusta National Golf Club in Augusta, Georgia; Round Hill Country Club in Greenwich, Connecticut; the Los Angeles Country Club; and the New York Yacht Club, to name just a few. Country clubs and athletic clubs exist all over the United States, so you should become familiar with the ones in your community. The list of members is rarely public information, so the prospect will have had to reveal this to the fundraiser or library director or have included it in a publicly available bio for you to find it out. You also may not be able to find information on the membership fees and dues for the club, but it is definitely worthwhile to look, as these types of members are often a very good indicator that your prospect is wealthy. Sometimes fees are reported via news sources, so be sure to check.

Board Memberships at Profit Organizations

When you find out that your prospect is on a company's board and he or she is not an employee of the company, then this membership requires a little more research. (Refer to chapters 5 and 6 for more information on employees' compensation.) Serving on a company board is not a volunteer position; board members are compensated through stock awards and salaries.

Once you determine that your prospect is a board member of a company, the first step is to see if the company is public or private, because this will indicate how much information you will be able to find on the stock holdings and salary awarded to your prospect for serving on the board. (Refer to chapter 7 for more information on stock and compensation from public companies.) To determine whether or not a company is public, search for the company on Yahoo! Finance (http://finance.yahoo.com) or another source that provides stock prices on public companies. If the company is listed, then it is a public company. If it is not listed, then it is private. You can find out if a company is private or public by searching Hoover's (www.hoovers.com) or another business reference source. You will also want to find out what the company does, to include that information in the research profile.

You will not be able to find the stock holdings or salaries for board members of private companies, so although being on the board of a private company is very likely to be an indicator of wealth, you will not be able to find compensation information. But otherwise it is valuable information to include in the research profile.

Board memberships at private companies will be found through the company's website or in a public bio on the prospect. Some private companies do not make the names of their board members publicly available.

Professional Organization Memberships

Determining if an organization is a professional affiliation for your prospect is a judgment call and is based, in part, on the profession of your prospect. The American Library Association is an example of a professional organization, as are the American Society of Appraisers and the American Bar Association. Professional organizations also may be for profit or nonprofit. You will find affiliations and memberships to professional organizations either through a publicly available bio on your prospect or you may also find this information directly on the website of the organization. Larger organizations will not necessarily list members on their websites, but they typically list their board members if they have a board.

You should review the size of the organization to determine the likelihood of members knowing each other. For example, the American Library Association's (ALA) executive board members know each other, and members of the same ALA committee probably know each other, but it is far less likely that individual members of ALA will know each other, as there are nearly sixty thousand members of the American Library Association.

How to Use this Information

There is overlap between many of the categories of organizations and clubs described in this chapter. The categories are meant only as general guidelines to help you determine what is significant about the prospects' membership or affiliation and what other lines of inquiry you might need to pursue in your research on the prospect. For nonprofit organizations that your prospect or your prospect's spouse/partner is affiliated with, also look for gifts from your prospect or spouse/partner to the organization. If the organization is for profit, then you will want to find, if possible, how much it costs to be a member of the organization. This might be another indicator of wealth for your prospect.

If you have found that there are library board members, volunteers, or donors who are also affiliated with the same organization, determine how likely it is that they would know each other. Take into consideration what role your prospect has in the organization, as board members and committee members probably would know each other. If the organization is small, members are more likely to know each other. All this information will be useful for your library director and fundraising staff.

Research Profile

In the research profile, include all the memberships and affiliations that your prospect and his or her spouse/partner have. You should include the roles they have in the organizations or clubs as well.

It will help your library director or fundraiser when reading the profile if you group similar types of organizations and clubs together in the profile; affiliations with nonprofit organizations should be grouped together, and for-profit organizations should be listed together. If it is not obvious, you will want to also include a brief description of what the organization is or does, meaning the mission of the organization. If the organization is a nonprofit, then list any gifts that your prospect or prospect's spouse/partner made to the organization. If you do not find any gifts, especially when the prospect (or spouse/partner) is on the board, then you may wish to include that information as well.

If the organization is for profit, list membership fees or dues for the organization, especially for golf clubs, private clubs, and country clubs, if you can find them. If it is board affiliation for a company, then state whether the company is private or public. This will indicate to your library director or fundraiser that you checked this. If the company is public, then also include stock holdings and compensation (described in chapter 6).

Don't include the number of members of the organization in the profile, but check this information prior to writing the profile, as this will help you to determine if you should also list in the research profile any volunteers, donors, or trustees of your library who are likely to know your prospect through membership or board membership to the same organization or club.

PRACTICE EXAMPLE 1

Your library director heard that a donor is a member of the board of trustees of the Walters Art Museum in Baltimore. The library director would like you to confirm this.

- You look at the Walters Art Museum's website. The board of trustees is listed under "About" and then "Governance" on the website.
- Next, you review the board members and confirm your donor is on the board.

PRACTICE EXAMPLE 2

Your fundraiser found out that a library prospect is a member of the Shriners. She would like to know what kind of organization that is and what is required to join it.

- You look at the national website for the Shriners—which is Shriners International and not the local chapter website for this information—where you will find that this is a fraternal order. You also search the Shriners organization through the IRS to confirm that this is a lodge.
- What is required to join is also described on the website, under "How to Become a Shriner."

PRACTICE EXAMPLE 3

Your library director finds out through a meeting with a prospect that the prospect is a member of a country club in your community. Your library director would like you to include in a research profile on the prospect how much it costs to be a member of the country club and if there are any library trustees who are also members.

- You look at the country club's website to find out if information is provided on member's fees or dues. This is very often not provided, and in fact the country club does not list that information.
- You search for news articles, using the search terms of the country club and membership fees or costs (and any similar searches). When that does not turn up anything, you see if you can find a general article about average costs to join a country club. You can use this amount if you can't find any other information.
- Unfortunately, finding other members of the country club is likely to be even more difficult, as that information is not likely to be provided by the club. With that in mind, you still try news and Internet searches using the names of your trustees and the name of the country club as search terms. You do not find any information.

- You also try searching in Marquis Who's Who under your trustees' names and the name of the country club as a keyword. Some people list their country club memberships in their bios.
- You include in the research profile that the prospect is a member of the country club, which you discovered in Who's Who, and any library trustees who are also members and the membership fees or dues. (If you could not find this information, then you would mention that in the research profile: "Information on the country club's membership fees and dues could not be found through available sources. The names of other country club members could not be found through available sources." This lets your library director know that you looked for the information.)

ONLINE SOURCES

Fee-based

Foundation Center .... **www.foundationcenter.org**
Allows searching by trustee name to find nonprofit board memberships. Foundations and grant-making nonprofit organizations are what will be found using this source.

GuideStar .... **www.guidestar.org**
Allows searching by trustee name to find nonprofit board memberships. Charities and foundations can be searched using this source.

Hoovers .... **www.hoovers.com**
Business reference source used to check whether companies are public or private.

Marquis Who's Who .... **www.marquiswhoswho.com**
Provides biographical information on prospects, possibly including club, professional, corporate, or fraternal order affiliations and memberships, as well as nonprofit memberships and affiliations.

Free

Internal Revenue Service .... **www.irs.gov/Charities-&-Non-Profits/**
Exempt-Organizations-Select-Check
Allows you to verify that an organization is a nonprofit. (You will find more information on this topic in chapter 7).

Yahoo! Finance .... **http://finance.yahoo.com**
Used to determine whether a company is public or private. Public companies' ticker symbols and share prices are listed through this site. (For further information on public companies, refer to chapter 6.)

MEMBERSHIPS AND AFFILIATIONS WORKSHEET TEMPLATE

CONFIDENTIAL

PROSPECT'S NAME:

Researcher's name: Date:

PROSPECT

MEMBERSHIP/AFFILIATION ORGANIZATION #1:

Organization address (city, state):

Prospect's role in organization (e.g., member, board member):

Type of organization: for profit   nonprofit

Mission or function of organization (e.g., golf club, art museum):

Membership fees or dues: $

Gifts given to organization: $

Source(s):

Notes:

MEMBERSHIP/AFFILIATION ORGANIZATION #2:

Organization address (city, state):

Prospect's role in organization (e.g., member, board member):

Type of organization: for profit   nonprofit

Mission or function of organization:

Membership fees or dues: $

Gifts given to organization: $

Source(s):

Notes:

MEMBERSHIP/AFFILIATION ORGANIZATION #3:

Organization address (city, state):

Prospect's role in organization (e.g., member, board member):

Type of organization: for profit   nonprofit

Mission or function of organization:

Membership fees or dues: $

Gifts given to organization: $

Source(s):

Notes:

PROSPECT'S SPOUSE/PARTNER

MEMBERSHIP/AFFILIATION ORGANIZATION #1:

Organization address (city, state):

Spouse's/partner's role in organization (e.g., member, board member):

Type of organization: for profit   nonprofit

Mission or function of organization:

Membership fees or dues: $

Gifts given to organization: $

Source(s):

Notes:

MEMBERSHIP/AFFILIATION ORGANIZATION #2:

Organization address (city, state):

Spouse's/partner's role in organization:

Type of organization: for profit   nonprofit

Mission or function of organization:

Membership fees or dues: $

Gifts given to organization: $

Source(s):

Notes:

MEMBERSHIP/AFFILIATION ORGANIZATION #3:

Organization address (city, state):

Spouse's/partner's role in organization:

Type of organization: for profit   nonprofit

Mission or function of organization:

Membership fees or dues: $

Gifts given to organization: $

Source(s):

Notes:

Capacity Ratings

AFTER YOU HAVE gathered all the wealth indicators that you were able to find for your prospect and your prospect's spouse/partner, you will use that information to come up with a capacity rating. A capacity rating is a way to compare prospects. It is a monetary value because it is based on wealth indicators. This rating is used to compare and rank prospects and to indicate whether or not they have the potential to be a major gift donor. The information gathered while doing prospect research is turned into a measure to compare your prospects to each other and to rate them. The purpose of a capacity rating is to identify who out of your library's pool of prospects are the wealthiest. Your library director and fundraisers can focus their attention on the prospects with the highest capacity ratings who should be able to give the largest gifts to your library.

Capacity ratings are a simple way to group and compare prospects using the information that you found while doing prospect research. You are identifying the prospects who are the wealthiest people in your prospect pool based on the very limited information that you are able to find. It is important to understand that the information you are using is not comprehensive. Nevertheless, what you have can be used as a rating system to compare prospects to each other.

Capacity ratings can be confusing because you will come up with a monetary value. It will look as if the capacity rating is the amount that a prospect is able to give to your library, and it is tempting to interpret a capacity rating in this way—but this is absolutely not the case. It is only a value to use for rating and comparison, and nothing more than that. For example, imagine that you were trying to put together a champion basketball team, but you had no information other than the heights of the players. Because you have no other information, the tallest players are more likely to be better basketball players than the shortest ones, so you would want to invite the tallest players to try out first. At the tryouts it would be up to the coach to determine whether or not those players were good basketball players by watching them play. In this example, the capacity rating is a person's height, and your library director or fundraiser is the coach. The library director or fundraiser need to build a relationship with the prospects to further determine how likely they are to give to the library and at what level.

What a Capacity Rating Can't Do

To make it a little easier to understand, it is important to know the limitations of what a capacity rating is and what it can tell you about your prospect. The amount of information that you will be able to find on your prospect and his or her spouse/partner is only a tiny fraction of his or her financial information. Most financial information is not publicly available. Your prospect's accountant or the Internal Revenue Service could come up with a much more accurate picture of your prospect's wealth than you can, but most people aren't willing to share this information publicly.

To add to this confusion, the term *capacity rating* implies that you know the actual capacity a prospect has to make to charitable institutions. Even though this is the term that is most commonly used in prospect research for rating prospects, it is a misnomer because you will not be able to determine a donor's capacity; you will not have enough information on your prospect to make this determination. Nevertheless, many prospect research departments define the capacity rating to mean the actual amount that a prospect could give in charitable contributions to all nonprofits organizations he or she might donate to over five years. This is not by any means verifiable information or even particularly useful. Your library director and fundraiser don't want to know how much a prospect will give to all nonprofit institutions; they are only interested in how much a prospect will give to your library. It makes it seem as if you just need to do one more calculation to give them the answer that they want. If you could provide this figure then you certainly would do so, as it would be invaluable to your library director and fundraisers, but you can't.

There is a much easier way to explain capacity ratings that will not be so confusing to you and your library director or fundraiser. If you think of a capacity rating merely as a system to rate prospects rather than a method to determine how much prospects will give, this confusion will be avoided. The capacity rating also will not take into account the prospect's affinity or likeliness to give to your library. It is up to the library director or fundraiser to build a relationship with the prospect and determine if the prospect will give to the library and at what level. Keep this in mind as you start to create and use capacity ratings.

Family Foundations

The exception to these caveats is the family foundation. As explained in chapter 7, you can predict that a family foundation will give approximately 5 percent of the foundation assets to other nonprofit organizations. This is a legal requirement and the only instance where you can determine this information. Unlike other measures, family foundations give you all the information you need to know. You can provide this information for a family foundation, assuming that the foundation will give the entire 5 percent distribution to your library. It is up to the library director or fundraiser to work with the prospect to get some or hopefully all of the distributions from the foundation for the year.

Creating a Capacity Rating

You have a few options to select from in creating a capacity rating system. These are based on some commonly used formulas used by prospect researchers in the field. The key thing is to select one option and stick to it, using it with all your prospects rather than using more than one method. There already will be many inconsistencies with using one method, so avoid adding more confusion to the process by using more than one method for creating capacity ratings. Read through the suggestions below and select your preferred capacity rating formula—or feel free to modify it, as long as you stay consistent.

The first rule for all the methods is that the capacity rating is based on the prospect *and* his or her spouse/partner; the rating is based on the household. Refer to the "Research Profiles" sections in previous chapters for more information on what you will use as the wealth indicator.

Capacity Rating Formulas

Capacity Ratings Based on the Largest Wealth Indicator

Using all the wealth indicators you can find for your prospect and your prospect's spouse/partner, take 5 percent of whichever wealth indicator will give you the highest value or amount, and use this figure for the capacity rating. For example, you would compare the market value of the property holdings, with salaries and stock holdings or net worth, if your prospect's (or spouse's or partner's) net worth is listed on a wealthy list. If there is a family foundation, then compare the foundation assets to the other wealth indicators. Take 5 percent of each to determine which wealth indicator will give you the highest rating. Following the rating amount, you should state what it was based on, such as property or stock holding. Refer to the worksheet at the end of the chapter to see how this is done.

The advantage to this method are that it can be used for prospects who have only one asset that you can find. This method will also work well for prospects who have publicly reported stock holdings and a modest home (rare, but not unheard of), because you are basing the rating on whatever will give you the highest rating. The issue with this method is that it weights prospects with more publicly available assets at a higher level than prospects with less publicly available assets, because you will be able to find more wealth indicators for prospects with more publicly available assets and will have more choices, which will increase the rating level.

Capacity Ratings Based on the Total Found Assets

The other option is to add together all the wealth indicators that you were able to find on your prospect and the spouse/partner and take 5 percent of the total to use as a rating. So, that would include property holdings, salaries, stock holdings, and family foundation assets. If your prospect has a published estimate of his or her net worth listed in Forbes or another source, then you would use just the net worth figure and take 5 percent of it for the capacity rating. The reason for this is that the net worth was derived from a person's assets, so if you combine it with the other indicators, you are counting those assets twice.

The advantage of this system is that it includes everything you can find, which seems more comprehensive. It also accounts for a published net worth figure for your prospects, if there is one. The drawback of this method is that it weights prospects with more publicly available assets at a higher level than prospects with less publicly available assets.

Capacity Ratings Based Only on Property Holdings

To base a capacity rating on property holdings, total the market value of all the property holdings owned by your prospect and his or her spouse/partner and take 10 percent of that total. That is the capacity rating. The reason it is 10 percent instead of 5 percent is because it is assumed that the property isn't the only asset, so traditionally a higher percentage is used.

A benefit of using this method is that property holdings are the easiest wealth indicator to find. Another advantage is that it limits the increased rating of prospects who have a lot of publicly available information on their wealth over prospects who do not. A drawback with using this method is that there isn't a very large range of home values at the very highest end of the housing market. So, if you have an extremely wealthy prospect, such as someone who is included on a *Forbes* wealthy list, he or she will have a similar capacity rating to someone who just has a very big house. In other words, if a prospect has a net worth of $5 billion and owns a house worth $5 million dollars, this is only 0.1 percent of his or her net worth.

Capacity Ratings Based Only on Salary

You can use the total salary for your prospect and his or her spouse/partner and take 10 percent of it to use the capacity rating.

The benefit to this method is that when you find actual salary amounts, you are able to differentiate between very high salaries, such as the top 10 percent from the top 1 percent of earners in the United States. It is a more granular method when you can find exact salary amounts. The downside is that for most people you will have only a range, and you will have to decide where to put them in that range to get a total to determine the capacity rating.

Capacity Rating Based Only on Giving

Total all the giving you can find from your prospect and his or her spouse/partner to other nonprofit institutions; calculate the average size gift to use as the capacity rating.

The upside of this method is that it is based on gifts, so it seems to make a little more sense than basing the rating on an asset or assets. The drawback to this method is that you will not be able to find all the gifts made by your prospect and his or her spouse/partner. Another thing to consider is that you may not be able to find gifts from all your prospects, and you will not be able to rate any prospects without gifts.

Family Foundation Assets

Unlike capacity ratings based on found assets, family foundation assets are the one measure you can actually use to determine how much a prospect could give to your library. Family foundations must give approximately 5 percent of their total assets as donations every year. (Refer to chapter 7 for more information on this subject.) Therefore a little extra consideration is required when you find that your prospect, or his or her spouse/partner, have a family foundation. Although you cannot guarantee that your library would be able to receive the entire 5 percent of assets, this is different from all the other wealth indicators in that it is an actual amount that your library could get.

You have a couple of options for how to incorporate this information into a capacity rating. You could select the first two capacity rating methods that incorporate family foundation assets into the rating. These are the methods that use or compare all the wealth indicators; namely, the capacity rating based on largest wealth indicator and the capacity rating based on total found assets. If you use any of the other rating methods based on only one wealth indicator that do not include family foundation assets, then you can separately flag prospects with a family foundation for your library director and fundraisers.

Putting Prospects into Ratings Tiers

Once you have a number of capacity ratings set for your prospects, you may wish to group prospects together in tiers so that similar ratings are grouped together. This can help if you are overwhelmed by the number and range of capacity ratings. An example of this would be to group prospects with capacity ratings ranging from $100,000 and higher in tier one, which would be your highest rated prospects. Prospects with ratings from $99,000 to $50,000 would be tier two; and so on. You would not be able to set the ranges for tiers until you have a number of prospect ratings completed to determine the range of your prospect pool—which are the top tier and which are the bottom. Ideally you would have between three and five tiers, divided into capacity range amounts: tier one would be your top tier prospects and the last tier, either three or five, would be your lowest rated prospect.

Wealth Indicators in the Research Profile Not Factored into the Capacity Rating

The wealth indicators for organization and club affiliations and political contributions may be included in the research profile—if you are able to find that information on your prospects—but these indicators are not necessarily factored into the capacity rating. The reason is you very often will not be able to find membership fees for golf clubs, country clubs, or private clubs, which are the types of membership fees that would be a wealth indicator. Political contributions to candidates have a cap on the amount individuals can give. Gifts to nonprofits have no upper limit for gift amounts and therefore are a better indicator of wealth than political contributions. If you find a wealth indicator that is very significant and not included in one of the capacity rating formulas described in this chapter, then add it using either of the first two methods described that factors in all wealth indicators.

That said, everything that you find about your prospect's wealth or his or her partner's or spouse's wealth should be included in the research profile. There may be several wealth indicators that you can't actually account for in a capacity rating, such as the sale of a private company where you do not know how much your prospect received for the sale, which will often be the case. Even if you are not able to factor this information into the capacity rating, it is important for your library director or fundraiser to know about it.

Wealth Screening

For a fee, the entire process of creating capacity ratings can be done for you. There are many companies that will screen your prospect pool or part of your prospect pool and match your prospects to their wealth information and provide ratings for them. This service is called a wealth screening. Prices vary, but the services can be quite expensive. It is an automated process, so you will still need to verify the information found through the screening, as sometimes the wealth information is matched to the wrong person.

Basically, the way a wealth screening works is that your library would forward data about your prospects to a vendor and through an automated process the vendor matches property holdings, stock holdings, salary information, nonprofit donations and all of the information that can be found on your prospects using public sources. The information is returned to you with the prospects' wealth information added in. A wealth screening saves a considerable amount of time, because the process is done for you or is very nearly done for you. Because it is an automated process, you will have to go through a verification process to make sure that the information attributed to your prospects was correctly attributed. There can be an issue with common names when a computer program is doing the research. Some of the companies that provide this service are WealthEngine (www.wealthengine.com), DonorSearch (www.donorsearch.net), DonorScape (www.donorscape.com), and Blackbaud (https://www.blackbaud.com).

Ask Amounts and Gift Officer Ratings

Many nonprofit organizations use more rating types than just capacity ratings. The two other most frequently used ratings are ask amounts and gift officer ratings. The ask amount is exactly what it sounds like: the amount the prospect was or will be asked to give to the institution. The prospect researcher or librarian doing prospect research does not determine this amount. This should be determined by the fundraiser or the library director after having conversations with the prospect and getting a feel for the level he or she might be willing to give to the library.

The second type of rating, gift officer ratings, is a rating assigned by the fundraisers or library director after a relationship has been established with the prospect. It is what the fundraiser believes the prospect is able and willing to give after meeting with the prospect. This rating is used in conjunction with capacity rating. If a library director determines that a prospect is much wealthier than could be discovered through prospect research, then the officer rating will be higher. If the fundraiser determines that the prospect is not willing to give very much to the library, then the officer rating will be lower. Specific suggestions for how to create these ratings is beyond the scope of this book. Sources you can consult to learn more about these ratings are included in the annotated bibliography (appendix B).

CAPACITY RATINGS WORKSHEET TEMPLATE

CONFIDENTIAL

PROSPECT'S NAME:

Researcher's Name: Date:

*Select **only one** of the five options below for all prospects.*

OPTION 1: CAPACITY RATING BASED ON LARGEST WEALTH INDICATOR

PROPERTY #1 ADDRESS:

Current value of property: $

Type of value (market or assessed):

PROPERTY #2 ADDRESS:

Current value of property: $

Type of value (market or assessed):

CO-OP ADDRESS:

Estimated value or actual value of prospect's unit: $

Total value of all property holdings: $

CAPACITY RATING BASED ON ALL PROPERTY HOLDINGS (×5%): $

EMPLOYER'S NAME #1:

Salary: $

Salary type: range   estimate   exact figure

EMPLOYER'S NAME #2:

Salary type: $

Salary type: range   estimate   exact figure

Total Value of Salary Amounts: $

CAPACITY RATING BASED ON SALARIES (×5%): $

NET WORTH

Amount: $

Source(s):

CAPACITY RATING BASED ON NET WORTH (×5%): $

PUBLIC COMPANY NAME:

Common Stock (total number of shares of directly held):

Current value: $

CAPACITY RATING BASED ON STOCK (×5%): $

FOUNDATION NAME:

Foundation assets: $

5% of foundation assets: $

LARGEST WEALTH INDICATOR:

CAPACITY RATING BASED ON (PROPERTY, STOCK, SALARY, ETC): $

OPTION 2: CAPACITY RATING BASED ON TOTAL FOUND ASSETS

PROPERTY #1 ADDRESS:

Current value of property: $

Type of value (market or assessed):

PROPERTY #2 ADDRESS:

Current value of property: $

Type of value (market or assessed):

CO-OP ADDRESS:

Estimated value or actual value of prospect's unit: $

TOTAL VALUE OF PROPERTY HOLDINGS: $

EMPLOYER'S NAME #1:

Salary: $

Salary type: range   estimate   exact figure

EMPLOYER'S NAME #2:

Salary: $

Salary type: range   estimate   exact figure

TOTAL VALUE OF SALARY AMOUNTS: $

PUBLIC COMPANY NAME:

Common Stock (total number of shares of directly held):

Current value: $

FOUNDATION NAME:

Foundation assets: $

NET WORTH (only use this figure for capacity)

Amount: $

Source(s):

TOTAL: $ **×5%: $**

CAPACITY RATING: $

INCLUDES FAMILY FOUNDATION ASSETS?   YES   NO

BASED ON NET WORTH?   YES   NO

OPTION 3: CAPACITY RATING BASED ONLY ON PROPERTY HOLDINGS

PROPERTY #1 ADDRESS:

Current value of property: $

Type of value (market or assessed):

PROPERTY #2 ADDRESS:

Current value of property: $

Type of value (market or assessed):

CO-OP ADDRESS:

Estimated value or actual value of prospect's unit: $

TOTAL VALUE OF PROPERTY HOLDINGS: $ **×10%: $**

CAPACITY RATING: $

OPTION 4: CAPACITY RATING BASED ONLY ON SALARIES

EMPLOYER'S NAME #1:

Salary: $

Salary type: range   estimate   exact figure

EMPLOYER'S NAME #2:

Salary: $

Salary type: range   estimate   exact figure

TOTAL SALARY AMOUNTS: $ **×10%: $**

CAPACITY RATING: $

OPTION 5: CAPACITY RATING BASED ONLY ON NONPROFIT GIFTS

RECIPIENT ORGANIZATION:

Amount of gift: $ Date of gift:

RECIPIENT ORGANIZATION:

Amount of gift: $ Date of gift:

RECIPIENT ORGANIZATION:

Amount of gift: $ Date of gift:

RECIPIENT ORGANIZATION:

Amount of gift: $ Date of gift:

RECIPIENT ORGANIZATION:

Amount of gift: $ Date of gift:

RECIPIENT ORGANIZATION:

Amount of gift: $ Date of gift:

TOTAL GIFT AMOUNTS: $

TOTAL NUMBER OF GIFTS:

AVERAGE GIFT AMOUNT: $

CAPACITY RATING (BASED ON AVERAGE GIFT AMOUNT): $

The Research
Profile

THE CULMINATION OF your prospect research
work is the research profile. After researching your
prospect and his or her spouse/partner, you will take
all the information you find externally through public sources
and internally from your library and use it to write a research
profile. The research profile is the report for your library director and fundraisers to learn about the library prospects'
backgrounds, interests, and wealth information, with the
goal of cultivating them to solicit them for gifts to the library.

A research profile includes all the information that you
have found on your prospect, his or her spouse/partner, and
their family. This information, used in conjunction with the
capacity rating, will give your library director or fundraiser
a great jumping-off point for starting or furthering a relationship with the prospect. The purpose of prospect research
and the product of the research is the research profile. The
research profile gives your library director or fundraiser the
information they need to select the best potential donors, and
the information in the profile should help your fundraiser
turn potential donors into donors to your library. Keep this
in mind as you are writing the research profile.

Writing the Research Profile

Use the research worksheets you have put together while researching your prospect to help you write the research profile
on your prospect. You can use either a research profile form

or a narrative style to convey the information about your prospect to your library director or fundraiser. Examples of both are included in this chapter. Feel free to modify them in whatever way is most useful to you and your library director or fundraiser. Further explanation of how to write research profiles are included in this chapter, and more directions are included within the templates.

To determine your preference for a narrative format or a form, try using both the form and using a narrative format to compile a research profile on the same prospect; do this for the first few prospects you research. Once you have established which format you prefer, stick with it and don't alternate between one or the other. This information is being compiled for your library director or fundraisers, and just as you will be learning how to write them, your library director or fundraisers are learning what is contained in them and what to expect. This is why the format should be consistent across all your profiles.

Narrative-Style Research Profile

One way to write a research profile is in a narrative format (see figure 11.1). Using some basic guidelines and being consistent with the order that you present information, you describe in complete sentences the information that you found on your prospect, his or her spouse/partner, and their family.

A great feature of the narrative style is that it allows for a lot of flexibility. You can include the information that is important, and you also have room for further explanation where it is needed. You also should include information that will make the research profile easy to read and understand. Don't get too bogged down in making sure to include every piece of information that you find if it isn't important or won't be informative to your library director, or if the information is obvious.

One drawback to using a narrative style is that your library director or fundraiser must rely on you to have done a thorough job in your research. In the narrative style you will probably not explicitly state that you looked for information you could not find on a prospect or that the information is irrelevant.

Form-Style Research Profile

The information in a research profile can also be presented using a template or form (see figure 11.2). By using your research worksheets as a guide, it is a very simple process to cut and paste the information directly into the research profile form. Delete irrelevant sections from the form as you complete it, such as the section for a maiden name for your male prospects, and delete from the section for the spouse's or partner's name, the word *spouse* or *partner* to make it clear what the relationship is. (Take a glance at figure 11.2 to see what is meant by this.)

Add extra sections if you need them, such as for a former spouse's name. Modify the template for each prospect to make it as efficient as possible to convey the information you need to convey about your prospect.

The benefit to using a template or form is that it works as a kind of checklist for all the pieces of information you will look for on your prospect, his or her spouse/partner, and their family. The issue with a form or a template is that it is somewhat less flexible and readable than the narrative style.

What To Include in a Research Profile

With your completed worksheets in hand, you will start compiling your research profile. You may find that you prefer to fill in the worksheets and write the research profile at the same time. Use whatever method works best for you. A research profile, whether it is in a narrative style or in a form, is usually divided into two sections: the first is the background on the prospect and his family, and the second section is on the prospect's wealth information. The categories of information that you will include in the research profile are listed below—information you find by following the methods and using the resources described previously in the book.

In the research profile, you will also want to include the prospect's affiliation with the library if he or she has one (e.g., trustee or volunteer) and information on the prospect's giving to your library. Include his or her giving, the spouse's or partner's if that was given separately, and any giving made through a family foundation, trust, or any other entity for which your prospect received an acknowledgment from your library.

Biographical Information

In the biographical section of the research profile, include the full name of the prospect and the partner's or spouse's full name and maiden name if you can find it. You should include their ages and birth dates as well. You will also include the schools attended, degrees earned, and graduation years for your prospect and his or her spouse/partner. Include information on the prospect's children and his or her spouse's or partner's adult children, if you can find that information. Include the names, ages, and background information of the prospect's parents and the spouse's (or partner's) parents, to let your fundraiser or library director know if the parents are alive and if there is any information about their wealth that might have some bearing on your prospect's wealth.

Next, include the business title and employer of your prospect and of the spouse/partner. Include a brief description of the company where your prospect works and where the spouse/partner works. Mention any pertinent information about the company, such as that the prospect is the owner of it. At this point you can also mention whether the company is public or private, its sales numbers, or any other relevant information.

Memberships and Club Affiliations

In the research profile, include all the memberships and affiliations that your prospect and his or her spouse/partner has that you can find. Include the name of each organization and the role your prospect and prospect's spouse/partner has in it, such as board member or committee member. Also include a brief description of what the organization is or what it does.

Group nonprofit organization memberships and affiliations together, and group for-profit organization memberships and affiliations together. List any membership fees or dues for golf clubs, private clubs, and country clubs, if you can find them. Company board memberships for your prospect or his or her spouse/partner should include the name of the company, what the company does, and if it is a public or private company.

Additionally, mention any fellow board members or club members who are library trustees, volunteers, or donors who are likely to know your prospect through their mutual membership or affiliation with an organization.

Real Estate

Include all the properties owned by your prospect or your prospect's spouse/partner. Mention the full address and the market value of each piece of property. You can also include the basic terms of the mortgage and the down payment for each property, if you were able to find that information. Also mention any property that was recently sold by your prospect, as well as the sales price and the date of the sale.

Salaries and Net Worth

In the research profile, include the salary or the salary range for your prospect and his or her spouse/partner, and the year the salary or salaries were earned. For exact salary figures, state the source of the information as well. For a salary range, if it is possible to determine this information, indicate where your prospect (or spouse/partner) is likely to fall within it; for example, at the high end of the range or at the low end. If your prospect or his or her spouse/partner is listed on a wealthy list with an estimated net worth, then include this information, along with the source, publication year and where he or she is ranked on the list (if the list is ranked by net worth).

Stock and Compensation from Public Companies

For your prospects who are corporate insiders at public companies, include in the research profile their compensation information: base salary and total compensation, listed as two separate figures. Be sure to include the name of the SEC document and the date in the profile. Include how the prospect will be compensated if he or she leaves the company; or you can wait to include this information once the prospect has left the company. Include the prospect's stock holdings as separate totals for directly held common stock, indirectly held stock, stock options, restricted stock, and phantom stock, along with the SEC documents and dates used to find this information. State the number of shares held of each type of stock and the value of the stock. (Remember that only *directly held* stock is used for the capacity rating.) For restricted shares, phantom stock, and stock options, include the vesting dates as well.

Family Foundations

For a family foundation affiliation, include in the research profile the name of the foundation, the address of the foundation, and the board members and their relationship to the prospect, if you can find that information. Include the foundation assets and the date of the 990 tax return. Include the total giving amount made by the foundation for that year as well. List the recipients of gifts and the amounts (unless that is a very long list, in which case you can just list the largest gifts). Be sure to also mention donations made by the prospect or his or her spouse to the family foundation.

Giving to Other Nonprofits and Political Contributions

List the gift amounts or gift ranges, the years the donations were made, and the institutions that received the gifts for all gifts that you can find for your prospect and your prospect's spouse/partner. If the name of the organization does not indicate what it is or what it does, then you may wish to include a brief explanation of that as well. For a prospect (or spouse/partner) who is on the board of a nonprofit organization, be sure to mention gifts that you find from your prospect (or spouse/partner) to that organization, and also mention it if you do *not* find any gifts made to the nonprofit.

For political contributions, list all the political contributions that you find for your prospect and your prospect's spouse/partner. Include the candidate who received the contribution or the PAC and the party affiliation, the amount of the contribution, and the year it was given.

Capacity Rating

You will select one capacity rating formula to use to rate all your prospects. The options are: capacity ratings based on the largest wealth indicator or based on total found assets, which are both calculated at 5 percent; capacity ratings based on property holdings, calculated at ten percent; capacity ratings based on salaries, also calculated at 10 percent; or capacity ratings based on giving to other nonprofits, which are based on the average gift size. State the capacity rating and what it was based on if it isn't clear. If you are also using tiers, then mention both the capacity rating and the tier in the research profile.

Gifts Made to the Library and Prospect's Affiliation with the Library

Although this information can easily be found by your library director or fund-raiser, you should include in the research profile the prospect's affiliation to the library (trustee or volunteer) and any giving to the library. Legal credit for a gift is determined by whose name is on the check, so you can break down the giving totals by who received legal credit for the gift (meaning, who gave the donation), which would include the prospect, the prospect's spouse/partner, a family foundation, or a donor-advised fund. Another option is to add all the gifts together for which the prospect received some acknowledgment from the library. That is, if your prospect received a thank-you letter from the library director for a gift made by his or her donor-advised fund (the prospect's name would not be on this check), then you can add that giving with the prospect's giving as one total, or you can list those giving amounts as separate totals. Look at the form-style template (figure 11.2) for further clarification. Ask your library director for his or her preference on this as well.

Storing Research Profiles and Worksheets

If your library has a donor database with the capacity for you to store research profiles in it, then do store them within the donor database. This may restrict your choices for the format of your research profiles. Most donor databases will allow only text, so you will probably have to use the narrative format for research profiles.

If your library does not have a donor database, then you will have to store your research profiles and worksheets on a secure network drive with limited staff access or a password-controlled individual computer, so that there is restricted, controlled access to this information. This is due to the sensitive nature of the research; you would not want a library patron to accidentally come across a research profile on a trustee of the library—or worse, on himself or herself. (Refer to chapter 1 for reminders on confidentiality policy.)

You should not send research profiles or worksheets to your library director or fundraiser as e-mail attachments, as this is not a secure process; an approved staff member could accidently forward such e-mail to someone who is not supposed to see it, as well.

For any paper files of your research profiles, and for any backup documentation that you have (such as SEC filings or property records), be sure to store such information in a locked, secure area. Shred any documents that you do not need to retain, and be sure to never keep worksheets, research profiles, or any research materials on your prospects on your desk or in a place where someone who is not supposed to see it could stumble across it.

FIGURE 11.1 RESEARCH PROFILE NARRATIVE TEMPLATE

CONFIDENTIAL

RESEARCH PROFILE NARRATIVE TEMPLATE

Below is an example of what you might include in a research profile. Feel free to include as much or as little as requested by the library director. In any event, all your sources should be listed on the worksheets. You have room in this format to add any additional information you find in a seamless way.

The bio and family sections are first.

Johnson is the maiden name.

Other information on his parents does not add any relevant information about his potential wealth, so it is not included.

This kind of detail lets your library director know that you looked for that information.

Employment information is next.

Law firms are not public companies, so the fact that this is not a public company is not explicitly stated, but do add this information for other companies and whenever you need to clarify this.

You can add former titles to this section, if you found that information.

It is very unlikely that your library director will not know what Yahoo is, so you can leave the company description out if it is unnecessary.

John A. Prospect is 42 years old. He was born in March 1971. He attended Duke University and earned a BS in 1994. His wife, Beth T. (Johnson) Prospect, is also 42 years old and was born in May 1971. Ms. Prospect attended Brown University and earned a BA in English in 1993 and an MBA from Harvard in 1997.

Mr. Prospect's parents are Jim and Mary Prospect. Birthdates and ages could not be found for them through public sources. Ms. Prospect's parents are Fred and Mary Johnson. Fred Johnson was born in 1945. He is 68. Mary Johnson was born in 1947 and is 66. Mr. Johnson was the owner and CEO of a large textile manufacturing firm, ABC Textiles, from 1980 until he sold the company in 2010 for an undisclosed amount.

John Prospect is an attorney with Smith and Smith law firm in San Francisco. The law firm specializes in estate planning and wills. The firm's reported revenue for 2012 totaled $75 million. Mr. Prospect joined Smith and Smith as an associate in 2000.

Beth Prospect is the chief financial officer of Yahoo. Ms. Prospect joined Yahoo in 2010. Yahoo is a public company with 2012 annual sales of $4.99 billion. Prior to joining Yahoo, Ms. Prospect was the CFO of Widgets Corporation, a company that makes and manufactures widgets.

Affiliations and memberships are listed next:

> Nonprofits are listed first, for-profits second.

> This gives your library director a heads-up to follow up with Mr. Robertson directly about this, if that is appropriate.

Real estate holdings are given next.

Salary and stock information is listed next.

> Give salary information for all salaries.

> If you find a piece of information that your library director will wonder how you found it, mention the source too.

> If she wasn't a corporate insider, you would want to mention that here or right after her employment information.

> You can add the share price here as well, if you prefer to do so.

> Refer to chapter 6 for more information on stock and compensation from public companies.

Family foundation is listed next.

> You would look for gifts to Rotary because you found out that the Prospects are members of it. If you did not find gifts to Rotary, then add a sentence about that fact here.

Mr. and Ms. Prospect are members of the Rotary Club of San Francisco. Rotary is a service club. Philip Robertson, a trustee of the library, is also a member of the Rotary Club of San Francisco. It could not be determined if Mr. Robertson and Mr. and Ms. Prospect know each other.

They are also members of the San Francisco Golf Club. Membership fees and dues could not be found for the club through public sources.

Mr. and Ms. Prospect own their home at 1515 Main Street in San Francisco, California. The current market value of the home is $2 million.

According to the *American Lawyer*, average salaries for partners earned in 2012 at Smith and Smith law firm totaled $450,000.

As a corporate insider at Yahoo, Ms. Prospect earned a 2012 base salary of $300,000 and a total compensation package of $1,000,000 (SEC filing DEF14A, 9/1/2013). According to the same SEC filing, Ms. Prospect directly held ten thousand shares of Yahoo stock with a current value of $340,000. She also has five thousand stock options, with a purchase price of $24 per share, and a vesting date of January 1, 2016. The current approximate value of the stock options total $50,000.

Mr. and Ms. Prospect are on the board of the Johnson Family Foundation, located in San Francisco. The most recent 990 tax return for the foundation is from 2012. Fred Johnson and Mary Johnson, Beth Prospect's parents, are also on the foundation's board. The 2012 foundation assets were $5,010,300 and foundation giving totaled $250,515. Recipients of the five largest gifts were the San Francisco Museum of Modern Art ($25,000), the San

Francisco Zoo ($20,000), the San Francisco Symphony ($10,500), the Chinese Historical Society of America ($10,000) and Rotary International ($8,000).

Nonprofit giving and political contributions are listed here.

Again, if you did not find gifts to the Prospects' member organizations, then add a sentence about that fact here.

Your library director will know that the president is a Democrat, so no need to state that.

Mr. and Ms. Prospect gave between $1,000 and $2,000 to the Chinese Historical Society in 2011. Ms. Prospect gave $50 to Rotary International in 2012.

Mr. Prospect gave $250 to Barack Obama's presidential campaign in 2012. Ms. Prospect gave $250 to Republican Jamie Wright's state congressional campaign in 2012.

End with the capacity rating, followed by the giving to the library and any affiliations to the library.

The highest wealth indicator is the capacity rating method that was used to calculate this.

Mr. and Ms. Prospect's capacity rating of $250,515 is based on their family foundation assets.

From 1999 to 2014, Mr. and Ms. Prospect have given a total of $10,000 to the library. Mr. Prospect is trustee of the library.

FIGURE 11.2 RESEARCH PROFILE FORM TEMPLATE

CONFIDENTIAL

Researcher's name: Date:

BIOGRAPHICAL INFORMATION

PROSPECT'S NAME:

Maiden name:

> Include the first name, middle name or initial, and last name.

Birth date: Age:

Schools attended, degrees earned, graduation years:

> e.g., Ohio State University, BA, 1975; Harvard Law School, 1980, JD

SPOUSE'S/PARTNER'S NAME:

Maiden name:

> Delete "Spouse's" or "Partner's" from the form when filling it in to confirm relationship.

Birth date: Age:

Schools attended, degrees earned, graduation years:

Adult children's names and ages:

Prospect's mother's name and age:

Prospect's father's name and age:

> Be sure to mention if either parent is deceased.

Brief background on parents:

> This section is to provide any wealth information that may have an impact on the prospect. E.g., Mr. Smith's net worth was estimated to be $35 million in 1980 by Forbes.

Spouse's/Partner's mother's name and age:

Spouse's/Partner's father's name and age:

Brief background on parents:

EMPLOYMENT INFORMATION

PROSPECT'S BUSINESS TITLE:

Employer:

Employment dates:

Type of business: e.g., bank, private company

Annual company sales: $

Brief background on career or past employment:

> This section provides further information on the prospect's previous employer if it is relevant to his or her wealth. E.g., Ms. Jones was the CEO of a large, private corporation from 1990 until 2000.

SPOUSE'S/PARTNER'S BUSINESS TITLE:

Employer:

Employment dates:

Type of business:

Annual company sales: $

Brief background on career or past employment:

PROSPECT'S NONPROFIT MEMBERSHIPS AND AFFILIATIONS

ORGANIZATION'S NAME AND MISSION: e.g., Milwaukee Museum of Art, art museum

Prospect's affiliation with organization: e.g., trustee or member

Library board members, volunteers, and donors who are also members:

Don't include this if it seems very unlikely that they would know the prospect. If included, add as many extra lines as needed to account for all nonprofit memberships and affiliations.

SPOUSE'S/PARTNER'S NONPROFIT MEMBERSHIPS AND AFFILIATIONS

Organization's name and mission:

Spouses's/Partner's affiliation with organization:

Library board members, volunteers, and donors who are also members:

PROSPECT'S FOR-PROFIT MEMBERSHIPS AND AFFILIATIONS

ORGANIZATION'S NAME AND MISSION: e.g., the Club at Boca Pointe, country club

Prospect's affiliation with organization:

Membership fees or dues: $

You can indicate here that you looked for this information but were unable to find it; e.g, Not found through public sources.

Library board, volunteers, and donors who are also members:

SPOUSE'S/PARTNER'S FOR-PROFIT MEMBERSHIPS AND AFFILIATIONS

Organization's name and mission: e.g., Target Corporation, public company*

Spouse's/Partner's affiliation with organization: e.g., corporate board member*

Membership fees or dues: $ Delete this if it is not relevant to the organization.

Library board, volunteers, and donors who are also members:

*A corporate board affiliation at a public company indicates that there should also be stock holdings and compensation in that section of the form below.

REAL ESTATE

PROPERTY #1 STREET:

City:

State:

Country: | Delete this if it is the United States. |

Property type: | e.g., home, condominium, co-op |

Mortgage information, purchase price, purchase date:

| | e.g., 30-year fixed, purchased in 1995 for $300,000; include this if you can find it, add more details if you found them, or delete this section. |

Current market value of property: $ | Change this entry to assessed value when necessary. |

| | Add as many lines as needed to account for all the properties. Most prospects will have only one property. |

SALARIES

PROSPECT'S SALARY: $

Exact salary or range   Salary year: | Compensation from a public company is in another section of the form. Use this section for all other salaries. |

SPOUSE'S/PARTNER'S SALARY: $

Exact salary or range   Salary year:

NET WORTH

PROSPECT'S NET WORTH: $

Source: | e.g., the Forbes billionaires list | Source date: | list published date |

Ranking on list: | Delete this entry if your prospect did not appear on a wealth list. |

SPOUSE'S/PARTNER'S NET WORTH: $

Source: Source date:

Ranking on list:

PUBLIC COMPANY COMPENSATION AND STOCK HOLDINGS

PUBLIC COMPANY NAME:

Ticker symbol:

Current share price: $

Directly held common stock:

number of shares

Stock value: $

This is what you will use for your capacity rating, if the rating is based on stock.

Indirectly held shares of common stock:

number of shares

Indirectly held shares value: $

Stock options:

number of shares

Options purchase price: $

Current options value less purchase price: $

Options vesting date:

Restricted stock:

number of shares

Current restricted stock value: $

Restricted stock vesting date:

Phantom stock:

number of shares

Current phantom stock value: $

Vesting date:

SEC filings and dates:

Base salary: $

Total compensation: $

Year of salary:

Retirement package information:

Delete this entry if it is not relevant.

Add as many lines as necessary to account for all public company affiliations or delete this section if it does not apply to your prospect or his or her spouse/partner.

FAMILY FOUNDATION

FOUNDATION NAME:

Address:

990 tax return date:

Board member's name, relationships to prospect: | e.g., Frank Miller, brother |

Board member's name, relationships to prospect:

Board member's name, relationships to prospect:

Board member's name, relationships to prospect:

Donations from prospect, spouse, or partner to foundation: $

Most recent foundation assets: $ | based on the 990 tax return |

Total giving from foundation in filing year: $

Recipient name and amount:
| e.g., Metropolitan Museum of Art, $1,000 |

Recipient name and amount:

Recipient name and amount:
| Add as many lines as appropriate to convey the largest gifts made by the foundation. |

Recipient name and amount:

NONPROFIT GIFTS (AND JOINT GIFTS MADE WITH THE SPOUSE/PARTNER)

RECIPIENT NAME, ORGANIZATION TYPE, AMOUNT OR RANGE, AND DATE:

| e.g., Metropolitan Museum of Art, Art Museum, $1,000 to $2,000 given in 2003 |

| Add as many lines as necessary to account for all gifts that you found. |

NONPROFIT GIFTS MADE BY THE SPOUSE OR PARTNER

Recipient name, organization type, amount or range, and date:

> Add as many lines as necessary to account for all gifts that you found.

POLITICAL CONTRIBUTIONS

Candidate's name or PAC name:

Political affiliation:

Amount of contribution: $

Date:

> Add as many lines as necessary to account for all gifts that you found.

POLITICAL CONTRIBUTIONS MADE BY THE SPOUSE OR PARTNER

Candidate's name or PAC name:

Political affiliation:

Amount of contribution: $

Date:

> Add as many lines as necessary to account for all gifts that you found.

CAPACITY RATING

Capacity rating: $

> Add what the rating is based on if that is not apparent.

Tier rating:

> Include this entry if you use this; otherwise delete it.

AFFILIATION AND GIFTS

Prospect's affiliation with the library:

_____

PROSPECT'S GIFTS TO THE LIBRARY

Total of prospect's gifts: $ _____

Total of spouse's/partner's gifts: $ _____

Total of prospect's family foundation gifts: $ _____

Total from prospect's donor-advised fund: $ _____

> Aside from the prospect's gifts he or she made directly, include any other gifts for which the prospect received a thank-you letter or some acknowledgment from the library.

TOTAL OF ALL GIFTS: $ _____

> Determine if your library director would rather see the giving broken out as it is above or as one sum.

_____

_____

> Add as many lines as necessary for any gifts made by other entities that your prospect received some acknowledgment for, such as his or her company.

Now you have all the tools and skills you need to provide prospect research for your library director or fundraising staff. With some practice you will find that prospect research is interesting and effective way to identify the best prospects for your library. Good luck!

APPENDIX
ONLINE RESOURCES
AND ANNOTATED
BIBLIOGRAPHY

A LIST OF online resources and an annotated bibliography is provided so you can find more information on prospect research and on general nonprofit and fundraising resources. The general fundraising resources and books are included to help you with the rest of the fundraising process, which falls outside the scope of this book.

This list of prospect research resources is different from the list of resources included at the end of the chapters in this book. Many of these web pages contain unique resources, so you will want to review and become familiar with them and create a favorites list to use for prospect research. You should also read the other books on prospect research to give you a more complete picture of the field. The annotations for the books include titles of the chapters to give you a better sense of what subjects each volume contains.

Online Resources

Prospect Research Online Resources

ORGANIZATION

APRA International
www.aprahome.org
> APRA is the membership-based professional organization for the field of prospect research. Many states have local chapters of APRA. APRA hosts annual conferences; provides online training and webinars; and publishes the online journal, *APRA Connections*, which focuses on prospect research and related topics. APRA also maintains a listserv for prospect researchers, PRSPCT-L. You do not need to be a member of APRA to subscribe to the

listserv. To join PRSPCT-L, refer to APRA's web page www.aprahome
.org/p/cm/ld/fid=87.

TRAINING AND GUIDES FOR PROSPECT RESEARCH

Blackbaud's "Prospect Research for the Non-Researcher," by David Lamb
https://www.blackbaud.com/files/resources/downloads/WhitePaper
_ProspectResearchForTheNonResearcher.pdf
> This document provides a brief overview of prospect research for
> development professionals who are not prospect researchers. It also includes
> a list of prospect research resources.

NOZA's "Training—for the New Researcher"
https://www.nozasearch.com/fundraising-resources.asp?!=1
> Included on this page is the "Prospect Research Workbook," a downloadable
> PDF document that provides an excellent overview of the prospect research
> process, suggestions for sources, and very useful research tips and tricks. This
> page also includes a downloadable template of a research profile.

PROSPECT RESEARCH RESOURCES LISTS

Aspire Research Group
www.aspireresearchgroup.com/links.html
> This consulting firm's web page provides a comprehensive list of prospect
> research resources organized under subject headings.

David Lamb's Prospect Research Page
www.lambresearch.com
> Provides a list of expert David Lamb's favorite prospect research resources.
> Also has links to blogs and general resources.

Michigan State University's Prospect Research Resources
http://staff.lib.msu.edu/harris23/grants/prospect.htm
> Provides links to resources used for prospect research and an excellent list of
> general prospect research resources and links.

Northwestern University's Research Bookmarks
www.nudevelopment.com/research/bookmark.html
> This comprehensive site provides links to resources used for prospect
> research, including sources used for international research.

Stanford University Development Research
www.stanford.edu/dept/OOD/RESEARCH

Provides links to resources used for prospect research. It also contains an extremely useful FAQ/help section for commonly asked prospect research–related questions. Link categories include Planes, Yachts and Horses; Salary Calculators and Lists; Online Profiles; Relationship Mappers; Political Contributions; and Prospect Research Blogs.

University of Southern California
www.usc.edu/dept/source

Links to prospect research resources are organized under three broad categories: Corporate Internet Research, Foundation Internet Research, and Individual Research. There is a list of general resources provided as well.

University of Vermont Prospect Research and Reference Tools
www.uvm.edu/~prospect

Provides a list of the university's favorite prospect research resources and links to commonly used resources used for prospect research.

University of Virginia's Portico: Web Resources for the Advancement Professional
http://indorgs.virginia.edu/portico/home.html

Prospect research sources are organized under general categories, including directories, biographical sources, property sources, and salary sources.

Wheaton College's Prospect Research Links
www.wheatoncollege.edu/Tools/ProspectResearch

Provides links to resources used for prospect research, including nonprofit locators and genealogy.

General Fundraising and Nonprofit Online Resources

ORGANIZATIONS

Association of Advancement Services Professionals (AASP)
http://advserv.site-ym.com

Membership-based professional organization for fundraisers that offers training and hosts an annual conference on fundraising.

Association of Fundraising Professionals (AFP)
www.afpnet.org

Membership-based professional organization for fundraisers and people working in the field. AFP holds an annual conference and also provides numerous in-person courses, e-courses, and webinars.

Council for Advancement and Support of Education (CASE)
www.case.org

Membership-based professional association for advancement professionals working at colleges and universities, as well as fundraisers working in other fields. CASE holds conferences and provides online courses and in-person training sessions, which are held all over the United States. CASE also publishes CURRENTS magazine and numerous other publications, which can be purchased directly through the website.

NONPROFIT AND FUNDRAISING ONLINE RESOURCES

Chronicle of Philanthropy
http://philanthropy.com

A journal that focuses exclusively on philanthropy, fundraising, and nonprofit topics. The *Chronicle of Philanthropy* website provides access to an interactive, comprehensive study, "How America Gives," based on 2008 individuals' tax returns. The tax returns are for the individuals' adjusted gross income, and the *Chronicle* also made additional adjustments to the income to calculate a figure for discretionary income. This study presents very interesting information, but you will not be able to determine an individual's adjusted gross income or their discretionary income, so be careful about trying to draw conclusions from this study about your prospects' overall giving.

Lilly Family School of Philanthropy
Indiana University–Purdue University Indianapolis
www.philanthropy.iupui.edu

Provides training courses and online training as well as producing the annual publication *Giving USA* on giving trends in the United States.

Annotated Bibliography

PROSPECT RESEARCH SOURCES

Filla, Jennifer J., and Helen E. Brown. *Prospect Research for Fundraisers: The Essential Handbook.* Hoboken, New Jersey: Wiley, 2013.

This book is written by Helen Brown, who has her own prospect research consulting firm, the Helen Brown Group, and Jennifer Filla, who also has a prospect research consulting firm, the Aspire Group. They are both well known in the field of prospect research. The audience for this book is gift officers and other fundraising professionals working within nonprofit organizations who are not familiar with prospect research. This book provides an overview of prospect research, explaining what the field encompasses. It also includes recommendations for hiring and managing a research department. This is an excellent book and will be invaluable to you as you start doing prospect research, as it puts the field of prospect research within the larger context of fundraising.

The chapters are: 1. The Big Picture; 2. Identifying New Prospects; 3. Researching Prospects; 4. Donor Relationship Management; 5. Managing Prospect Research; 6. Ethics, Risk, and Data Protection: What's the Big Deal?; 7. International Prospect Research; 8. Trends and Opportunities: The Future of Prospect Research.

Hancks, Meredith L. *Getting Started in Prospect Research: What You Need to Know to Find Who You Need to Find.* Rancho Santa Margarita, California: CharityChannel Press, 2011.

The audience for this book is prospect researchers who are new to the field, although it is also a very useful source for seasoned prospect researchers, as well. This volume provides an overview on how to do prospect research and an extensive list of recommended resources to use. This volume also includes a description of the day-to-day activities of the author, which will give you a great insight into what it is like to do prospect research. The author is the director of prospect research and management at Western Illinois University. This book will get you a long way in knowing what to anticipate as you begin to do prospect research.

The chapters are: 1. First Things First; 2. Terms of Endearment: Communicating with Frontline Fundraisers; 3. Find a Friend: Mentors and Helpers; 4. On the Lookout: Scanning for Prospects; 5. The Bubble-Up Philosophy: Data Mining, Modeling, and Screening; 6. Compiling Data: Locating and Verifying Information; 7. Profiling Jane Q. Donor: Putting it Together; 8. Research on a Dime: Inexpensive Resources; 9. A Day in the Life of Research; 10. Finding a Job in Prospect Research: Making Headway into the Field; 11. Wrapping it up.

Hogan, Cecilia. *Prospect Research: A Primer for Growing Nonprofits.* Sudbury, Massachusetts: Jones and Bartlett Publishers, 2008.

This is the most well-known book on prospect research; in fact, until very recently, this was the *only* book published on the subject. It is an extremely dense and comprehensive overview of the field. In addition, this book also includes examples of forms and templates used in prospect research and a very useful glossary of terms. This volume is owned by or has been read by most prospect researchers working in the field.

The chapters are: 1. The History, Evolution, and the Mission of Prospect Research; 2. A Good Time for Ethics; 3. Who Are the Prospects? Definitions, Process, and Tools; 4. Institutional Prospects–Corporations, Foundations, and Government Funding; 5. Research Math; 6. Philanthropic Capacity; 7. Building a Pool of Potential Prospects; 8. Electronic Screening; 9. Prospect Tracking; 10. Walking the Talk (or How to Be a Prospect Researcher); 11. Creating a Research Plan; 12. Development and Research: Living in the Development World; 13. Building a Prospect Research Reference Library.

Fundraising Sources

GENERAL FUNDRAISING

Bray, Ilona. *Effective Fundraising for Nonprofits: Real-World Strategies That Work.* Berkley, California: Nolo, 2010.

This book provides an excellent overview of fundraising. It has a very broad scope and contains a lot of practical information. The volume includes examples of fundraising forms, worksheets, sample letters, and marketing materials. It also provides a brief section on how to do prospect research on major donors.

The chapters are: 1. Your Fundraising Companion; 2. Fundraising Tools; 3. Developing Your Fundraising Plan; 4. Attracting Individual Supporters; 5. How to Keep the Givers Giving; 6. Midscale and Major Donors; 7. Funds from the Great Beyond: Bequests and Legacy Gifts; 8. Special Events; 9. Raising Money Through Business or Sales Activities; 10. Seeking Grants from Foundations, Corporations, and Government; 11. Creating Printed Communications Materials; 12. Designing Your Website to Draw in Donors; 13. Outreach by Traditional and Social Media.

Ciconte, Barbara L., and Jeanne G. Jacob. *Fundraising Basics: A Complete Guide.* Sudbury, Massachusetts: Jones and Bartlett Publishers, 2009.

This dense volume covers all the major topics related to fundraising and nonprofits. The print book provides templates, forms, sample appeals, and public materials, many of which can be found on the CD counterpart provided. This book also features a chapter on prospect research. Recommended resources are included throughout the book.

The chapters are: 1. Ensuring the Future of Philanthropy—An American Tradition—Through Accountability and Ethical Fundraising; 2. The Many Roles of Board, Staff, and Volunteers in Fundraising; 3. Building a Professional Development Operation; 4. Your Fundraising Database—A Tool for Success; 5. Developing and Evaluating Your Fundraising Plan; 6. Building Relationships for Your Organization Through Annual Giving; 7. Using Direct Mail, Telemarketing, and the Internet to Build a Donor Base; 8. Prospect Research; 9. The Use of Personal Solicitation in Major Gift Fundraising; 10. Corporate Fundraising; 11. Raising Money From Foundations; 12. Special Events—The Fun in Fundraising; 13. Fundraising Communications—Electronic and Print; 14. Capital Campaigns; 15. The Basics of Planned Giving; 16. Association Foundation Fundraising; 17. Fundraising with Affiliates or Chapters; 18. Working with Consultants: Hiring and Using Consultants in your Fundraising Programs; 19. Fundraising as a Career.

Reiss, Alvin H. *CPR for Nonprofits: Creative Strategies for Successful Fundraising, Marketing, Communications, and Management.* **San Francisco: Jossey-Bass, 2000.**

This extremely readable and well-organized book includes actual examples from nonprofit organizations, which are used to explain the process, from getting recognition for a nonprofit organization, to holding fundraising events and asking for gifts.

The chapters are: 1. Getting Your Message Heard; 2. Making Your Event Special; 3. Asking for Money; 4. Involving Your Board and Reaching Your Audiences; 5. Pursuing the Corporate Dollar; 6. Employing a Businesslike Approach; 7. Maximizing Your Grassroots Potential.

Tempel, Eugene R., Timothy L. Seiler, and Eva E. Aldrich. *Achieving Excellence in Fundraising.* **San Francisco: Jossey-Bass, 2011.**

This is the third edition of this classic work on fundraising, first published in 1991. This volume discusses in depth all of the major topics in the fundraising field, including prospect research.

The chapters are: 1. A Philosophy of Fundraising; 2. Plan to Succeed; 3. Developing a Constituency for Fundraising; 4. Developing and Articulating a Case for Support; 5.The Total Development Plan; 6. The Annual Fund; 7. Major Gifts; 8. Capital Campaigns; 9. Establishing a Planned Giving Program; 10. Contemporary Dynamics of Philanthropy; 11. Prospect Research; 12. Corporate Giving and Fundraising; 13. Foundation Fundraising; 14. Women as Donors; 15. High-Net-Worth Donors; 16. Ethnicity and Giving; 17. Giving

Differences among the Generations; 18. Personal Solicitation; 19. Direct Mail Marketing; 20. E-mail and Internet Solicitation; 21. Special Events; 22. Telephone Solicitation; 23. The Practice of Stewardship; 24. The Trustee's Role in Fundraising; 25.Volunteer Management; 26. Using Social Media to Energize and Mobilize Your Volunteers; 27. Managing the Fundraising Program; 28. Leadership and Team Building; 29. Organizational Strengths and Vulnerabilities; 30. Donor Database Management and Segmentation; 31. Budgeting for Fundraising and Evaluating Performance; 32. Marketing and Communications for Fundraising; 33. Selecting and Working with Fundraising Consultants; 34. Fundraising for Grassroots Nonprofits; 35. Ethical Frameworks for Fundraising; 36. The Law and Fundraising; 37. Fundraising as a Profession; 38. Fundraising Credentialing; 39. Preparing for the CFRE Exam; 40. International Perspectives on Fundraising; 41. Resources for Strengthening Fundraising.

ASKING FOR GIFTS

Fredricks, Laura. *The Ask: How to Ask for Support for Your Nonprofit Cause, Creative Project, or Business Venture.* San Francisco, California: Jossey-Bass, 2010.

This book, which has a broader focus than just fundraising, is an excellent tool to use to prepare you to ask for things, including donations and gifts from donors. The first half of the book prepares you to "make the ask," and the second half of the book gives guidance on how to do it. Practice exercises are included throughout to help you learn the process.

The chapters are: 1. What Money Means to You and Why Ask?; 2. Do You Have a Well-Thought-Out Plan of What You Want?; 3. How Do I Know Who to Ask and When to Ask?; 4. Who Should Make the Ask and in What Setting?; 5. Asking for a Cause—Small and Large Charitable Gifts; 6. Asking for Yourself; 7. Handling the Responses to the Ask; 8. Following Up with Each and Every Ask; 9. When the Answer Is "No" and When the Answer Is "Yes"; 10. Pulling It All Together.

Levy, Reynold. *Yours for the Asking: An Indispensible Guide to Fundraising Management.* Hoboken, New Jersey: John Wiley & Son, Inc., 2008.

Focusing on the subject that is the most difficult for many fundraisers—how to ask for gifts—this thought-provoking, encouraging work written by the former president of the Lincoln Center is based on his experiences in fundraising and asking for gifts from donors, foundations, and corporate donors. It is *his* manual on how to ask for gifts.

The chapters are: 1. Fundraising: A Call to Alms, a Call to Action; 2. Soliciting Individual Prospects; 3. Asking Face to Face; 4. The Institutional Donor: Corporations and Foundations; 5. Technique: Special Events and Direct Mail; 6. Tough Questions: Candid Answers; 7. A Passport to Successful Fundraising: Lessons of a Lifetime; 8. Humor and Fundraising; 9. Fundraising: Dimensions of the Future; 10. Questions That Matter.

PLANNED GIVING, ESTATE GIFTS AND BEQUESTS

Sharpe, Robert F. *Planned Giving Simplified: The Gift, the Giver, and the Gift Planner.* New York, New York: John Wiley & Sons, Inc., 1999.

This book provides a thorough explanation of the very complicated subject of planned gifts. It gives an overview of the different forms of planned giving. It also covers who gives planned gifts to nonprofits and why, and provides guidance for fundraisers on how to ask donors for planned gifts.

The chapters are: 1. An Introduction to Planned Gifts; 2. Current Planned Gifts; 3. Deferred Planned Gifts; 4. Who Makes Planned Gifts?; 5. Why People Make Planned Gifts; 6. What Planned Givers Want to Keep When They Give; 7. The Planners Who Help People Make Planned Gifts; 8. Charitable Gift Planners; Who They Are; 9. The Giver and the Charitable Institution Connection; 10. The Charitable Estate-Planning Drama; 11. Acknowledgments, Recognition, and Memorials; 12. The Role of the Board of Trustees in Making the Institution's Planned Giving Program More Effective; 13. The Role of the Chief Executive Officer and Senior Managers in Building a Planned Giving Program.

STARTING A NONPROFIT ORGANIZATION

Goettler, Jim. *The Everything Nonprofit Toolkit: The All-In-One Resource for Establishing a Nonprofit that Will Grow, Thrive and Succeed.* Avon, Massachusetts: Adams Media, 2012.

This is a great source whether or not you are starting a nonprofit. It explains all the concepts and processes of nonprofits, as well as providing valuable examples. The book includes a CD with the forms and documentation that are needed and used by nonprofit organizations.

The chapters are: 1. Organizer to Organizer: Let's Talk!; 2. Networking Within Your Community; 3. Understanding Organizations and Corporations; 4. The First Organizing Meeting; 5. The Initial Board of Directors; 6. Articles of Incorporation; 7. By-Laws; 8. Filing Incorporation Documents; 9. Record-

Keeping Systems; 10. Developing a Budget; 11. Bank Accounts; 12. Fundraising; 13. Board Development; 14. A Business Plan; 15. A Mission Statement; 16. Publicity and Outreach; 17. Staff; 18. Finally! The 1023; 19. Board Liability Insurance; 20. Operation Staff and the Board of Directors; 21. Personnel Issues; 22. Changing From a For-Profit Organization to a Nonprofit.

WRITING FUNDRAISING MATERIALS AND APPEALS

Browning, Beverly. *Perfect Phrases for Fundraising.* **New York: McGraw Hill, 2013.**

This useful little book is about how to write effective solicitation letters and use electronic and social media communication to raise funds for nonprofits. This volume also includes instructions on how to conduct successful telephone solicitations and provides directions for in-person solicitations as well.

The chapters are: 1. Perfect Phrases for Fundraising Letter Campaigns; 2. Perfect Phrases for Internet and Social Media Campaigns; 3. Perfect Phrases for Telephone and Face-to-Face Campaigns.

INDEX

A

accessibility, 11

accountability, confidentiality policy, 13

ACRIS (database), 37

advisory privileges, 78

affiliations and memberships

    prospects and, 3, 15–16

    research profiles and, 126

ages and birth dates, 19

agricultural organizations, 75

Algonquin Club, 101

Allyn Foundation, 72–73, 75

alumni as prospects, 4

American Association of Fund Raising

    Counsel (AAFRC), 12

American Lawyer (website), 43, 46, 47

American Library Association, 10, 103

American Medical Group Association, 43

American Red Cross, 99

Ancestry.com (website), 19, 20, 23

announcements, weddings and obituaries, 19

annual reports, 88–89, 99

APRA (organization), 7, 12–14, 141–142

Aspire Research Group, 142

assessed values, 33

Association for Healthcare Philanthropy

    (AHP), 12

Association of Advancement Services

    Professionals (AASP), 143–144

Association of Fundraising Professionals (AFP),

    12, 144

attorney's salaries, 43

Augusta National Golf Club, 102

B

bank account information, 5

Benevolent and Protective Order of Elks, 102

bill of rights, donor, 12, 14

biographical information, 5, 15–29, 125

birth dates and ages, 19

Blackbaud (database), 117, 142

Bloomberg (website), 66

board members, 2–3, 79

botanic garden libraries, prospects for, 4

Bureau of Labor Statistics Wage Data, 42, 47

business leagues, 75

C

calculators, mortgage, 34

capacity ratings

    research profiles, 127

        about, 111–113

ask amounts, 117
creating, 113
family foundation assets, 115
formulas, 113–115
templates, 118–121
tiers, 115–116
wealth indicators/screening, 116–117
CareerBuilder (website), 42, 47
Caxton Club of Chicago, 101
Cejka Search (website), 43, 47
Center for Democracy and Technology, 10
chapter clubs, 98–99
charities, public, 75
Chronicle of Higher Education (website), 44, 47
Chronicle of Philanthropy, 144
churches, donations to, 89
civic and service clubs, 100–101
civil servants salaries, 44
Cleveland Museum of Art, 89
clubs. *See* memberships and affiliations
CNN Money Mortgage Calculator (website), 38
co-ops, 35
codes, IRS nonprofit, 75
colleagues, researching, 3
Collegiate Times (website), 44, 46, 47
Columbia Club, 101
company websites, 17
compensation
alternative sources, 63
corporate insiders, 54–55
IPO's and SEC Form S-1, 63–64
online sources, 66–67
practice, 65
proxy statements, 55–60
public companies, 53–54
research profiles, 64, 137
SEC Form 3, 4, 5, 60–62
confidentiality policy
accessing research, 11
creepy factor, 9–10
donor bill of rights, 12, 14
ethical standards, 12–13

inclusions, 10–11
information sharing and, 6–7
informing staff and board, 2–3, 9–14
legal issues, 10
storing profiles, 11–12
writing, 12
conflicts of interest, 13
contributions, 127
corporate foundations, 75–76
Council for Advancement and Support of
Education (CASE), 12, 144
country clubs. *See* memberships and affiliations
county assessors, 31–32

D

databases, biographical information, 16, 18
David Lamb's Prospect Research Page, 142
defining inclusions, 10–11
doctors' salaries, 43
donors
donor-advised funds, 78–79
affiliated prospects, 3
bill of rights, 12, 14
databases, 11, 117
defined, vii
Internet searches, 88
researching, 2–3
DonorScape (database), 117
DonorSearch (database), 117
Dun and Bradstreet (database), 18, 23

E

e-mail addresses, privacy and, 5, 11
EBSCOhost (database), 88, 92
Edgar (website), 66
education
history and, 18
information regarding, 5
employment information, 5, 18, 43
encrypted information, 11

endowments, 88
EquilarAtlas (website), 66
ethical standards, 12–13
executives' salaries, 44–45
exempt organizations, 75
exemption status, 98

F

Facebook (social media), 21, 24, 64
fact-checking, 17
Factiva (website), 19, 23, 88, 92
faculty salaries, 43–44
fair market value, 33
family foundations
    990 tax returns, 76–77
    additional entities, 78–79
    capacity ratings, 113
    defining, 71–72
    finding foundations, 73–74
    operating, 75–76
    practice, 80–82
    private versus family, 72–73
    research profiles, 79, 127
family information, 5
family trees, 20–23
Federal Election Commission, 18, 22, 89, 91–92
fee-based sources
    biographical information, 23–24
    family foundations, 82
    memberships and affiliations, 106
    prospect donations, 92
    real estate, 37
    salaries and net worth, 47
    stock holdings and compensation, 66
feelings, research and, 9–10
files, storage, 11
501(c)(3) organization, 78–79
Flikr (social media), 21
Follow the Money (website), 89, 90, 92
Forbes (magazine), 35, 36, 41, 45, 48, 114
Forbes Wealthiest Zip Codes (website), 38

foreclosures, 34–35
foreign nonprofits, 74
form style, 124, 132–139
form 990-PF, 77
formulas, capacity ratings, 113–115
foundations, family, 71–85
Fouresquare (social media), 21, 24
fraternal orders, 99, 100
free sources
    biographical information, 24
    family foundations, 82
    memberships and affiliations, 106
    prospect donations, 92
    real estate, 37–38
    salaries and net worth, 47–49
    stock holdings and compensation, 66–67
Friends group members, 3

G

genealogical information, 20–21
general salaries, 41–45
gift officer ratings, 117
gifts
    Internet searches, 88
    to libraries, 128
    locating donors, 1
giving
    capacity ratings on, 115
    requirements for, 78
Glassdoor (website), 42, 48
grants
    990 tax returns and, 76–77
    foundations and, 71–72
    guidelines, 73, 76
Grantspace, 75, 88
Groiler Club of New York, 101
guidelines
    family foundations and, 73
    getting started, 3, 10
guides and training, 142
GuideStar (website), 43, 48, 73–74, 76, 78, 82

H

Health Career Center (website), 43, 48
Helen Brown Group (website), 45, 48
history and education, 18
Hoover's (database), 18, 23, 47, 66, 103
horticultural organizations, 75
households, ratings and, 113

I

inclusions
    confidentiality and, 10–11
    research profiles and, 125–128
Indeed (website), 42, 48
independent foundations. *See* family
    foundations
Independent Order of Odd Fellows, 102
information access policies, 5, 11
information sharing, 6–7
integrity, confidentiality policy, 13
internal information, 5
Internet searches, 21–22, 43–44, 88
IRS
    capacity ratings, 112
    charities & nonprofits online, 82
    codes, 75
    donor-advised funds, 78–79
    exempt organizations, 98
    family foundations and, 73, 82
    Form 990, 76–77
    990 tax returns, 76–77
    nonprofit codes, 75
    operating foundations and, 75–76
    Publication 526, 74
    section 501(c)(3), 75, 78–79
iWave (database), 36, 37

J

John D. and Catherine T. MacArthur
    Foundation, 73
Jonathan Club, 101

K

Knights of the Columbus, 102

L

labor organizations, 75
lawyer's salaries, 43
legal issues
    capacity ratings, 113
    confidentiality, 10
Lexis-Nexis for Development Professionals
    (database), 19–20, 23, 36–37
library type, research and, 3
Lilly Family School of Philanthropy, 144
LinkedIn (website), 18, 24, 98
Los Angeles Country Club, 102

M

maiden names, 20
MarketWatch (website), 66
Marquis Who's Who (website), 98
memberships and affiliations
    athletic and country clubs, 102
    board at profit organizations, 102–103
    boards and nonprofits, 99–100
    civic, service, private, social, et. al.,
        100–102
    for-profit clubs or nonprofit, 98–99
    nonprofit board members, 79
    online sources, 106
    practice, 105–106
    professional organization types, 103
    research profiles, 104, 126
    searching for, 97–98
    using information, 103–104
    worksheet templates, 107–109
Merritt Hawkins (website), 43, 48
Metropolitan Club, 101
Michigan State University's Prospect Research
    Resources, 142
Moose International, 102
Morningstar Document Research (website), 66

Mortgage Calculator (website), 38
mortgages, 33–34
mosques, donations to, 89
museum libraries, prospects for, 4
Museum of Fine Arts (Boston), 89
museums. *See* memberships and affiliations

N
narrative style, 124, 129–131
National Arts Club of New York, 101
net worth and salaries
    estimates, 45
    general salaries and compensation, 41–45
    research profiles, 126
New York Yacht Club, 102
news sources, 88
990 tax returns, 43, 74, 76–77, 78
nonprofits
    board memberships, 79, 99–100
    codes, 75
    online resources, 144
    organizations, 43
    research profiles, 127
North American Industry Classification System
    (NAICS), 42
Northwestern University's Research
    Bookmarks, 142
NOZA (database), 20, 24, 87, 88, 92, 142

O
obituaries, 19
Obituary Data (database), 19, 23
Office of Personnel Management (website),
    44, 49
O*NET OnLine, 42, 48
online sources
    annotated bibliography and, 141–144
    biographical information, 23–25
    family foundations, 82
    memberships and affiliations, 106
    prospect donations, 90–91

real estate, 37–38
research process, 5
salaries and net worth, 47–49
stock holdings and compensation, 66–67
OpenSecrets (website), 89, 92
operating foundations, 75–76
organizations, 143–144

P
paper files, confidentiality and, 11
parent institution, 3
parents of prospects, 20
patrons as prospects, 4
PC (public charities) code, 75
permissions, accessibility and, 11
permissions, policies and, 12
PF (privation foundation) code, 75
philanthropic information, 5
philanthropy, Bill of Rights and, 14
physicians' salaries, 43
Pinterest (social media), 21, 24
pledges, 88
POF (private operating foundations) code, 75
policies, 2, 5
political action committees (PAC), 89
political contributions, 89–90, 127
potential donor defined, vii
practice
    confidentiality policy, 13
    family foundations, 80–83
    memberships and affiliations, 105–106
    prospect donations, 90–91
    real estate, 36–37
    research profiles, 22–23
    salaries and net worth, 46–47
preamble, confidentiality policy, 13
presenting research, 2
principal salaries, 43–44
privacy
    companies and, 44–45
    information and, 5
    laws for, 10

social clubs and, 101

special libraries and, 4

procedures, 2

professional organization memberships, 103

profiles

company websites, 17

family foundations, 79

memberships and affiliations, 104

real estate, 36

salaries and compensation, 46

storing, 11–12

writing, 6

property holdings, 5, 32, 114

property records, 11, 32–33

Proquest (website), 19, 24, 88, 92

prospect giving

online sources, 92

other nonprofits, 87–89

political contributions, 89–90

practice, 90–91

research profiles, 90

worksheet templates, 94–96

prospects

affiliated, 3

comparing, 111

employers and, 18

research process, 1–7

resources, 142–143

public charities, 75

public companies

research profiles, 126–127

salary information, 44–45

public information, 4–6

public library prospects, 4

public officials salaries, 44

Publication 526, 74

Q

QFinance (website), 66

R

real estate

co-ops, 35

county assessors, 31–32

mortgages, 33–34

property records, 32–33

research profiles, 126

trusts, 35

values, 33

worksheets, 39–40

zip codes, 35–36

religious organizations. *See* memberships and
   affiliations

research, prospect, 1–7

research profiles

biographical information, 21

capacity ratings, 111–121

creating, 123–139

family foundations, 79

form style, 124, 132–139

membership and affiliations, 104

prospect donations, 90

real estate, 36

salaries and compensation, 46

salaries and net worth, 46–49

writing, 6

Round Hill Country Club, 102

rules, operating foundations, 75–76

S

salaries and net worth

capacity ratings and, 114–115

estimates, 45

general and compensation, 41–45

privacy and, 5

research profiles, 126

Salary.com (website), 42, 49

searches, 97–98

SEC Form 4 Guidelines (website), 11, 66

section 501(c)(3), 75

service and civic clubs, 100–101

sharing information, 6–7
Shriners International, 102
social and private clubs, 101
social media sources, 21, 24–25
Social Security Death Index (database), 19, 24
social security numbers, 10
social welfare organizations, 75
special-interest clubs, 101
Special Libraries Association (SLA), 99
special or private libraries, 4
sponsoring organizations, 78–79
spouses and partners, 19–20
staff, 1–3
standards and guidelines, 10, 12–14
Stanford University Development Research, 143
stock compensation, 126–127
stock holdings
    corporate insiders, 54–55
    IPO's and SEC Form S-1, 63–64
    online sources, 66–67
    practice, 65
    proxy statements, 55–60
    public companies, 53–54
    research process, 5
    sources, 63
storing profiles, 11–12, 128
surgeons' salaries, 43
synagogues, donations to, 89

T

Tax Assessor Database, 37
tax-exempt organizations. *See* memberships
    and affiliations
taxes
    codes, 72
    form 990, 76–77
teacher salaries, 43–44
telephone numbers, 5
templates
    biographical information, 16, 25–29

capacity ratings, 118–121
    family foundations, 84–85
    form style, 124, 132–139
    memberships and affiliations, 107–109
    narrative style, 124, 129–131
    prospect donations, 94–96
    real estate holdings, 39–40
    salaries and net worth, 50–51
    stockholdings and compensation, 68–69
tiers, capacity rating, 115–116
total found assets, 114
trade associations, 75
training and guides, 142
trusts
    family foundations, 79
    nonexempt, 76
    real estate and, 35
    research process, 5
Twitter (social media), 21, 25

U

underwater mortgages, 34
Union League Clubs, 101
University of Southern California, 143
University of Vermont Prospect Research and
    Reference Tools, 143
University of Virginia's Portico, 143
university prospects, 4
U.S. Securities and Exchange Commission, 19
U.S. Tax Code, 72, 75
USA Jobs (website), 44, 49

V

values, finding, 33
volunteers, 3

W

Wayne State University, 88
wealth indicators, 75, 113–114

Wealth-X (website), 45, 47
WealthEngine (database), 16, 24, 117
wedding announcements, 19
Wheaton College's Prospect Research Links, 143
worksheet templates
    biographical information, 16, 25–29
    capacity ratings, 118–121
    family foundations, 84–85
    memberships and affiliations, 107–109
    prospect donations, 94–96
    real estate holdings, 39–40
    salaries and net worth, 50–51
    stock holdings and compensation, 68–69
    storing, 11
World Affairs Council, 101
writing
    confidentiality policy, 12
    research profiles, 6, 123–124

Y

Yahoo! Finance (website), 45, 49, 67, 103
Yahoo! Homes (database), 38
YouTube (social media), 21, 25

Z

Zillow (database), 36, 38
zip codes, 35–36
zoo libraries, prospects for, 4